EVIL
CORN

BOOKS BY ADRIAN C. LOUIS

POETRY

The Indian Cheap Wine Séance (1974)
Muted War Drums (Chapbook, 1977)
Sweets for the Dancing Bears (Chapbook, 1979)
Fire Water World (1989)
Among the Dog Eaters (1992)
Days of Obsidian, Days of Grace (1994)
Blood Thirsty Savages (1994)
Vortex of Indian Fevers (1995)
Ceremonies of the Damned (1997)
Skull Dance (Chapbook, 1998)
Ancient Acid Flashes Back (2000)
Bone & Juice (2001)
Evil Corn (2004)

FICTION

Skins (1995, 2002)
Wild Indians & Other Creatures (1996)

EVIL
CORN

Adrian C. Louis

ELLIS PRESS
Granite Falls, MN
2004

EVIL CORN

Printed in the United States of America.
Manufactured by Thomson-Shore, Dexter, Michigan.

ISBN 0-944024-52-1

10   9   8   7   6   5   4   3   2   1

Published by ELLIS PRESS
PO Box 6, Granite Falls, MN 56241
http://www.ellispress.com

ACKNOWLEDGMENTS

Some of the poems included in this edition have been published previously in *Ploughshares, Mississippi Review Online, American Indian Quarterly, Speakeasy, New Letters, Cedar Hill Review, Omega Online Journal, Talking River Review, Agenda* (England), *Red Rock Review, Solo,* and in the anthologies *SEPTEMBER 11, 2001: AMERICAN WRITERS RESPOND* (Etruscan Press, 2002), *HOW TO BE THIS MAN* (Swan Scythe Press, 2003), and *HORSES* (Seven Devils Press, 2004). The poem "Me and Simon Send Smoke Signals on the Great and Gaseous Internet" is copyrighted © 2004 by Adrian C. Louis and Simon Ortiz.

The author extends his sincere appreciation to Margaret Dalrymple and Trudy McMurrin, former editors at the University of Nevada Press, and to John Rezmerski for editorial suggestions. Special thanks to David Pichaske, Bill Holm and Marcy Brekken, Jim Northrup, Sandy Mosch, Buddy and Jeannette Tabor, Lucita Medrano, Robert Berner, and Leslie Silko who donated candles to light the peculiar darkness of southwest Minnesota.

*f*or Colleen, who can
no longer read these words . . .

⬚

Close your eyes,
I'll be here in the morning.
Close your eyes,
I'll be here for a while

— TOWNES VAN ZANDT

CONTENTS

Milking the Nightmares   **13**

Moving From Point A to Pointless   **14**

Evil Corn   **15**

The Death Scent of the Corn Plant   **17**

This Dirt in My Mouth   **18**

A Lack of Anything Remotely Magical in Stone-Cold Minnesota   **19**

From a Windowless Classroom at the College of the Corn   **22**

The Lump on Goggles' Neck is an Egg
with Baby Jesus Growing Inside   **24**

Goggles as Savior of Gizzard   **27**

At Pine Ridge Pow Wow Grounds   **29**

Lonesome Boners   **31**

Crows on MN County Road 61   **32**

The Reconstruction   **33**

The Crow Chronicles   **34**

Thanksgiving in the Promised Land   **37**

Minnesota Turkey Daze   **38**

On the Couch of November   **40**

Anonymous Dogcatcher Hotmail   **41**

Naming the Dance   **42**

Arse Poetica   **43**

Wisconsin   **50**

An E-Mail to Woody   **51**

Me and Simon Send Smoke Signals on the
Great and Gaseous Internet   **52**

God's Beard Is Caked With Campbell's
Chunky Chicken Soup   **54**

A Temporal Feline Distraction
Takes Its Claws to the Calendar **55**

Another Day in the English Dept.
or Meet Me at Medicine Tail Coulee **57**

Indian Woman Popcorn Prayer **59**

High Plains Bermuda Triangle **60**

Breakdown Boogie Dreams **63**

Hog Heaven: A Porcine Epistle **65**

Gaudeamus Igitur **68**

Grammatical Neanderthal **69**

Zoloft **71**

For an Indian Girl I Once Knew in my Stone-shaded
and Tumescent Past **72**

A Month After No E-mails, I Call Back East
and Learn You're Dead **73**

Plains Indian Riddle: June 25th **75**

Christmas Present **76**

Metaphorical Morlock, Minnesota **77**

A Hermit in a Blizzard **78**

Deer at my Kitchen Window **79**

Jazzly Inconsequentia **80**

Fata Morgana **81**

Another Deer at my Kitchen Window **82**

Explaining my Scream to the Nervous Stranger in my Bed **83**

Discarded Lines from a Lost Life: The 1964 High School
Yearbook and Its Sad Emission of Ghosts **84**

Blue Horse **88**

A Savage Among the Kids of the Korn **89**

Witch Wind **90**

Logorrhea **91**

Sister of St. Francis **92**

A Meditation on the Mexicanos in Southwest Minnesota **92**

Juneau Indian Riddle **95**

Small Town Vampires **96**

Is the Ace of Spades a Race Card? **97**

Apropos of Appropriation, Expropriation, and Expiation within this Great Nation **98**

A Miscellany of Now Dead Red Girls **100**

Calling the Cats **104**

His "Hollywood" Fantasies Produce a Vision of Daring Escape in Which He Discovers God Might Exist **105**

Meanwhile, Back at the Ranch **106**

In the Bosom of Abraham **107**

The Last Shall be First and The First Shall be Last or Something Similar **109**

Aurora Borealis **110**

Sun Dance **111**

The Obituary **113**

The Day the Jets Kissed the Twin Towers **114**

Liberty Street **115**

Post-Traumatic Skin Disorder **116**

Approaching the Double Nickel **118**

Recalling Days of Wine and Roses **119**

For the Black Horse of My Death **121**

Christmas Day 2003 in Nebraska **123**

That Indian I Hate Arrived Today **124**

Ghost Dance Song for Colleen **125**

About the Author **126**

Some of them knew pleasure,
some of them knew pain.
And for some of them it was only
the moment that mattered.

On the brave and crazy wings of youth,
they went flying around in the rain
and their feathers, once so fine,
grew torn and tattered.

— JACKSON BROWNE

MILKING THE NIGHTMARES

Dear love, dear sweet broken love,

Tonight I am swilling down the lunar anxieties of the pumpkin moon. Despite aging hands over fearful eyes, I can see the brief angle of angels, their panties of bright silk glued to strong hips. I can hear the red-eyed ghosts of buffalo in the prairie wind. The ugly, gaunt beasts are nuzzling old cottonwood twigs in the dry creek bed and mumbling in Indian.

Sweet, fractured woman, I give you this expectant oasis of waking dream. Take these sorrowful dances of ragged memory; take these merciless dandelions, these laughing, yellow songs of toughness mounting weakness. Here are the guns and the bullets, the infections and the pus. Sweetheart, these shallow words are my scars. They're all I have except the faint drum of our hearts tolling my ambiguous loss, and that low, muted thumping when we kiss in the piss-scented fog of your nursing home nightmare.

MOVING FROM POINT A TO POINTLESS

One year before the millennium, the fat American sun spits shards past the cedars and through my K-Mart Venetian blinds. A spirit voice on AOL *Instant Messenger* is using the magic word LOVE. This voice knows I love another who is dancing with a terminal disease, but this voice is desperate, confused, and Christ, it confesses to wanting to gobble my gonads over the Internet! I tell it pain lives around that corner. The spirit voice begs me to run from responsibility, asks me to apply to teach in its city. It thinks I'll do great—wants me to go from the minor leagues to Cooperstown. If that is love, it is an aberrant love. *Sometimes I think I'm being stalked, but I like it.*

This goes on for more than a year and I come to see there's nothing on earth so painful, so pitiful as middle-aged lonely lust. *Okay,* I tell the voice, *I love you, too.* Pathetic. Man, I am pathetic and more than twelve years sober, talking to a voice whose body I've yet to see. Nevertheless, I mail my résumé to its sparkling school on the Pacific coast, but at the last minute I accept a harvesting job at the College of the Corn, deep in the deadlands of Minnesota, a day's drive from bleak glyphs I've clawed onto the Dakota of memory.

EVIL CORN

My first few months in Minnesota, I listen to a Public Radio performer pimping a perfidious, nasal patter of prairie companionship, and I can't help but wonder what hairless planet he's nattering from. Okay, on the surface, it's safe here. Life *is* ordered. No stone-heart urban thugs a'dancing. No fearsome city noise to start the ears a'bleeding. But something about the place gives my bones the heebie-jeebies. Left to the sun and rain, this land of quaint squares of dark soil sprouts a bright uniform green from road to road that murders anything natural. Gone are the tall grass prairies, vanished are the native trees, and corralled are the once-feathered Indians. Evil corn and its masters have murdered this land.

I wake to my first harvest in southwest Minnesota and see that corn, the basic grain, the light of dark Indian stomachs for millennia, has transformed from a life sustainer to a life destroyer. When I tell a friend the corn is now evil, she titters and whispers, "Oxymoron." Transplanted city folk at the college say how glad they are to be away from cities and in "the country," but this place is not "the country" even though a green blanket shrouds the four sacred directions. This is subjugated land, strangely industrial and rural at the same time. Corn and soy fields rotate on alternating years. The corn here is tall and imposing, but it is not the same creature Squanto planted and spoon-fed the loony pilgrims with. This is not the corn of the Zuni *shalako,* and it's not the Diné holy giver of pollen.

This is not the corn I scratched into the dry dirt of my childhood. This is mutant flora, a green American Frankenstein born of chemicals and greed. It is lucre bound for the sweet tooth of America in the form of corn syrup, for our car gas tanks as ethanol, and as fodder for the stomachs of cattle. These cobs, genetically altered and pesticide soaked, cornhole all that is sacred.

In dreams I recognize the sacred, have always tried in my profane way to bow to the sacred, but waking decades of hand-to-mouth survival have nearly blanched all holiness from my soul. Despite my occasional frothing, a typically generic American consumer lives in my mirror. Yet I reside in an ancient farmhouse surrounded by evil corn. Green death rises from this bad-heart land where I've brought my cats and dogs. We're exiled to a toxic hell where the laughing devils of necessity have chased us, five hundred miles from the dying woman we love. Do not pity my animal friends or me. Pity the sallow and linear pimps who greedily grow green the destruction of our ancestors and their natural world.

THE DEATH SCENT OF THE CORN PLANT

Corn to the left of me—corn to the right. Into the valley of corn rode I with my Joad dogs and cats until I found an odd Oz, a blaring cornucopia belting out a blue fog of indifference disguised as the blue shine of heaven.

This is a dead land. This is a bad-heart-land. There is something rotten here in Morlock, Minnesota—there is no other way to describe the air except to say it smells like the 13,000 citizens of this corn-fed town convened hourly in the college stadium and passed gas at the same instant and topped it off by burping Grain Belt beer into the rising blue cloud of stink.

This is a putrid land. I believe the gene-spliced particulate matter from the Archer Daniels Midland Corn Plant in Morlock has created a colony of agrarian zombies, but now that I'm in residence, I guess I'll have to go with the flow and swim through the evil corn until I find me a zombie girl to bang. Oh, what a wonderful death *that* will be.

THIS DIRT IN MY MOUTH

The steaming, mosquito summer surrenders to a fall day. A cold fog stumbles in and whitewashes the map. Appropriate appropriation, this frosting of a ghost land. I fear this fog but not as much as I fear the ceaseless wind. The ass-kicking air shrieks that things in this soil are undeniably evil, things predating the spillage of wild Indian blood by any convenient mob of greedy white men. Some have told me that ancient Indians on their southern trek to the Pipestone quarries never camped near Morlock, that it was a "bad-spirit" place. Others have told me *yes*, there was a Dakota village site near here. I have tried to ask some of the nearby *Dakotapi* what the real story is but they only speak *mazaska*, the language of the slot machines.

Given no answers, I fall to the ground and root deep in the dead soil. I grasp dozens of evil spirits by the napes of their necks and spit them into the bleak sunshine. They smirk, give me the finger, and seep back into the dark, dark earth and I am left with nothing but the earthen mouth of a dirty, old man.

THE SAD LACK OF ANYTHING REMOTELY MAGICAL IN STONE-COLD MINNESOTA

I totter home, twitching from teaching the god-fearing students at the College of the Corn. I'm little more than a gray-haired wage slave, in exile from all my false selves, naked and slightly erect before all the pretentious and spermatic pyrotechnics of my youth. I *am* one of those now ancient fools who spent too many years lost in the rain of Juarez . . . On good days, I try to give students the crumbs of any illusory truths I've eaten. On bad days, I contrive temporal epiphanies to raise the grades of the unread, beautiful girls who march with rap music between their white thighs. I'm purely part of the economy and I could live with that if only I could hear a few brave hearts beat against the ribs of this skeletal land. But, almost everyone here seems to have sold out. Worse, I have finally had to eat the irony that poets are coveted by feckless and unavoidable dilettantes whose prime directive, aside from preserving their jobs, is to stick their hand into the dark hole of art and run away waving their fingers like bragging high school boys. I know someone once said the answer is blowing in the wind, but who—and why—and when did it matter?

Stone-cold Minnesota may be the death of me. I've told friends of dark shadows that dance in bright daylight here. Maybe the world *is* flat and I've fallen off the edge, tumbled down, ass bouncing into self-pity. Worried allies have sent obvious medicines: sage, cedar, and sweetgrass. A few have sent eagle feathers. I've told people of the screaming silence of fog that appears here with no warning. I've painted the omen of the swarming crows onto the ears of a few academic friends I work with, but they only shrug. More gifts flow in from the outside world. A tribal writer in the high nothing of Wyoming FedEx's me a chunk of obsidian streaked with the blood of love. A childhood friend from Nevada mails sacred magpie feathers from the soil I emerged from. My guilty rejection of true home shimmers sadly in their black sheen. *Dear cousin, forgive me in my dotage.*

Stone-cold Minnesota may be the death of me. And more medicine flows in. A witch from North Dakota sends a spell written on homemade paper, a sprig of mugwort, a boar's tooth, and tracts from the Order of Nine Angles, but I don't know if such white witchery works for semi-educated half-breeds.

An ancient poet-ally sends a fork of elk antler from Arizona's Mogollon Rim. I have drunk-driven the descent from Winslow to Payson under bone-light moon and I've seen the spirit elk. I place the antler against my ear and it whispers that there's more wildlife on the moon than on these bloodless Minnesota fields. I have been sent many medicines, and an ancient foolishness deep inside of me says if I array all these objects on the kitchen table and pray, then something good *is* bound to happen.

Something good is bound to happen? Better men than I have found no solace in that eternal prayer of the broken man. *Something good is bound to happen?* Will I be young again with my phalanx of eventual mistakes waiting to be courted and dueled with again? Half of me knows I'm just kidding myself, but the other half asks if middle age doesn't entitle foolishness? I know I'm only here counting my gray hairs and building my annuity, but just last week I clicked the heels of my K-Mart sneakers together three times and whispered: *There's no place like home.* Lost brothers like me will understand why I like the tribal taste of that phrase. *There's no place like home. There's no place like home.* But, I have no home no more. I live out of my farmhouse like a salesman lives out of a suitcase. And it isn't like this stretch of soil is any different than any other location in this forlorn nation. It's just that ancient human magic is totally dead here, and that's the way the fundamentalists want it. Sooner or later they will name this entire dying planet "America."

FROM A WINDOWLESS CLASSROOM
AT THE COLLEGE OF THE CORN

I.

Outside, a perky chill is in the air. Inside, there's a blind kid with a laptop and a yellow lab in the classroom and several blond girls are petting his huge, sleeping dog. While I read the syllabus aloud, I notice I've got a dime-sized chunk of skin missing from my forearm. It's oozing blood. I do not know how or when my battle wound occurred. Could've been at noon when I drove home to let the dogs out. Goggles, Rez-raised mutt and once the fastest dog I ever saw, lumbered across the lawn. Gizzard, mostly Pekinese, blind in one eye, deaf, and toothless, chased a fat rabbit into the pregnant cornfields and I waddled in after him. I must have been shanked by the late season cornstalks. Gizzard is getting senile. The blind kid's yellow lab is young, sleek, and healthy. I may steal him and gain myself some extra eyes. Hell, I might take his laptop too.

II.

Lord, this big, buxom Nigerian girl! After class, when I say her paper's weak, she squeaks at me in a startling way. Makes tiny African woman moans. I ask her if she's whining. She nods and makes more of the noises, makes eye contact until my bread rises. I ask her if she can cook. "Yes, I am a hot cook," she says. A *hot cook?* My ears steam and I twitch from head to foot, and just when I'm ready to ask her to come to my rustic farmhouse, the next professor to use the room rushes in, drops her heavy briefcase onto the desk, and glares at me like I was a pus-filled pimple on a pork-fed student.

I cram my papers into my bag, look for the ebony girl, but she is gone. The pallid, professorial shrew with a twitching blue eye and corn silk hair is tapping her foot and waiting. Sorry, I mumble and shamble away. I'm sorry—*you bloodless box of useless facts.* I'm sorry—*you dryfuck chunk of blue eye and sinew.*

THE LUMP ON GOGGLES' NECK IS AN
EGG WITH BABY JESUS GROWING INSIDE

One scrotum-shriveling winter night sixteen years ago I drove from Pine Ridge, SD to Rushville, NE to irrigate my dry liver. I farmed all night with the usual crew of suspects and some Skin I'd never met named Goggle Eyes. The next morning back at the C.C. Yards in Pine Ridge, I walked out into the yard to hock loogies and saw a shivering ball of dogflesh, a puppy that stank from a distance and had a rear rubbed raw from mange and fleas. She had a Lone Ranger mask, looked to be part terrier and the rest just Rez-blend humping. She was a painful sight for a parched brain, so I tried to shoo her far away.

Get lost! Go away you goggle-eyed excuse for a dog. I mean it. Scram, you red monkey-butt pup! There's no room in this here inn.

Colleen and I had four Indian mutts already, plus three cats, so I picked the puppy up and carried her a hundred yards down the road to the pow wow grounds. I sat her down by the creek and escorted my hangover home. When I reached our house, she was there with me, whining at my feet. I shut the gate of the chainlink fence with her outside, and went in for coffee. When I came back out that afternoon, she was still there with tragic eyes behind her dark mask on a white face—Lazarus returned from the dead. "Goggle Eyes go home," I grunted and left for Nebraska and the harsh medicine of the wild Indian bars. Hours later, hangover cured, I sped the weaving, red road home and let the little dog into my disheveled yard and life. Now, more than sixteen years later, Goggles, the second truest love of my life, has followed me to maudlin Minnesota where I believe the grim, demon shadows just might squelch our yelping souls.

Goggles, who once held the world record for the hundred-dog-reservation-dash, has developed a walnut under the skin of her neck. I think this seed is Jesus, waiting to be reborn. Holy Goggles, Mother of God, pray for us dogs in our hour of need. Goggles, goddamn it, we've got to abort the Lord. Kill that cretin before he climbs His cross and marks our loss for eternity.

After the biopsy . . .
Well, the local vet says, *It's not lymphosarcoma.* My hardening heart soars like so many clichéd eagles. I smile. *It's fibrosarcoma, which if anything, is deadlier,* she adds. Oh Goggles, what will we do? This thing is now egg-sized. You are the egg-man. You are the walrus. And I've brought you to this strangely fastidious yet hog-stinking prairie to breathe the last air we'll share.

During the Xmas break I drive west for seven hours and have our regular vet remove the awful thing. Days later

Goggles looks just great. She almost looks brand-new. When she spots a squirrel in our yard and gives chase, I am nearly moved to pray. The Jesus egg seems to have gone its alien way and decided to not return. *Maybe it has all been a horrible dream, or worse . . . a cheap preview of God's eventual scheme of rustic and callous débridement.*

Back in Minnesota, in early January I awaken to the leering viper of loss hissing into my face. I'm lugging Goggles down the three steps of the cement back porch and into the bitter snow every few hours to pee. She staggers constantly, her eyes are glazed, and with every one of her painful steps I pray for the guts to cap her. I tell myself, tomorrow, for sure, I'll call the vet to do her in, but I know I won't. I want to be cradling her the holy moment she slips into the sunlight of that bright and bounding field where old dogs chase new souls.

GOGGLES AS SAVIOR OF GIZZARD

One day I'm shuffling across campus, late for class, when the music begins. It's the saddest, honky-tonk redskin blues you ever heard, but only I can hear it. Every step I take is choreographed. Every step is strong and smiling. And as if my brain hadn't slopped enough cruel gruel onto my plate, I've now started to contemplate my own dying on a daily basis. *Lord, don't pity the poor poet and the sad and peculiar perks of his middle age. Death (and those fixations thereof) is in the first paragraph of his job description.*

Still, my scenarios of demise dance to and fro, but seriously shake a leg when I remind myself that there's not a single student of mine born before the fall of Saigon. Nary a one who could explain the whys and wherefores of Huey P. Newton. And it's not like I really know when or how I will end, and I guess I don't really give a rat's ass as long as I'm marching to a Delta blues beat. Maybe, one fine day I'll be strolling to class in a blizzard when the big one hits like a ten-pound sledge to the chest. Whether I croak or just get some veins Roto-Rootered, I'll have no worries because Goggles will drink from the toilet, standing on her withered haunches until she is sated, and then she'll belch water onto the floor so that tiny Gizzard can lap the sacred liquor of life. *This is a sweet, sappy reverie.* Goggles as savior of Gizzard is the dream of a romantic fool.

Today I realize that Gizzard, my ancient Pekinese, is going to outlive Goggles when I witness her rear legs give out and she falls, quivering onto the dull, gray carpet. Her eyes will not reflect me. She shivers and curls up next to me curled up on the couch. I smudge her with sage and call the vet for the coup de grace, but the vet is out tending pigs. I get up and drive into Morlock for some new .12 gauge shells.

When I get back an hour later, Goggles is stiffer than jerky. Gizzard is asleep, and he must have slept when the reaper came for Goggles with his rusty, rustic scythe. Outside, an inexorable sadness rises from the dead, blue soil and fouls my careless heart. I lie down on the rug and snuggle my dead little dog and try to remember something in the somewhere when young and strong, we were.

AT PINE RIDGE POW WOW GROUNDS

*Everything dies, baby that's a fact, but maybe
everything that dies some day comes back.*

— BRUCE SPRINGSTEEN

The bitter glue of snow makes the seven-hour trip take twelve. I'm crying—have been sobbing off and on for more than two days. I'm a pitiful, middle-aged mess. Goggles is in the trunk in a Hefty Bag, and Gizzard is snoring in Pekinese on the back seat. The red devil of drink is on my left shoulder, jabbering, railing against his cotton-mouthed banishment of twelve long years.

It's dusk when I hit the Rez and cruise into Pine Ridge Village. I pull past the softball field named for Colleen's brother Delmar and park at the pow wow grounds. Near a shabby stand of gaunt ash, I lay Goggles down like she's some sweet, enchanted princess, sleeping peacefully on a bed of new snow. In the time it takes to smoke a Marlboro, she is nearly covered with white crystal glitter. Corpulent tears, as bitter as I ever cried, waddle down my age-cracked face. In the midst of such appalling sadness, I force out a contemptuous snicker followed by a bone-rattling shudder. It's either that or fall down dead myself.

Oh Goggles, you're home now. Sixteen years ago we stood in this same exact spot, and then you followed me into my mangy life. What a flea-ridden, stinky, sad puppy you were. And what a crazed, wild ride lay ahead of us. Sleep now. Sleep little girl. When you wake in the spring, you'll really run fast. Yeah, you'll really run lickity-split. When you wake, the drummers will be drumming and the dusty dusk of the wacipi *will intoxicate us. Muscular and contemptuous young hip-hop Skins will be swaggering, pints and joints stashed in their back pockets. Your average* NDNZ *will be looking for hope like pitifully poor people across the globe do.* Sunka, *you can stay for the flag song, but then you must dance back home. Dance back through my tart and loving memories. Dance past this blinding bitterness blazing in my brain.*

I wipe the snow from her brow and kiss her nose. Then I drive away with Gizzard still snoring on the back seat of my senile Crown Victoria. The dirty streets of Pine Ridge carry me back to the squalor of my own youth. For an instant I'm young and the good, red road ahead is not dead, nor filled with holes that can swallow the soul.

LONESOME BONERS

Gizzard staggers to the front door, half asleep, tongue out, looking for his absent partner in crime. It is the same for me. I never would have thought I'd sleepwalk, but many nights now I awaken walking up the stairs. Some ulcerated region of my brain says Colleen's in bed upstairs, so I budge from the couch and trudge up toward the life we shared. When I'm half a flight up, I realize she's gone and gone forever. This happens several times a week, has been happening for seven years. Now Gizzard is doing the same dance. He barks, so I let him out into the biting, frozen gloom. On the icy tundra where Goggles always peed, he spins circles and howls. Five minutes later, he's at the door, whining to escape the cold. Inside, he looks me in the eye and shudders. We're two old curs, palsied by the foul scent of ghosts, but we are still alive. Despite graveyard blues, despite lonesome boners, we can still snarl and on some ethereal, yet-to-be stolen prairie, our ancestors smirk.

CROWS ON MN COUNTY ROAD 61

¿Los viste en el río?
Estaban allí para saludarte.
¿Te diste cuenta de que el indio de piel oscura
con los bolsillos vacíos que había en la ribera
abarrotada y estrecha,
sostenía una flecha rota?

— NEIL YOUNG

From this cheap prairie farmhouse I cannot see other dwellings. But in the blue sea of frozen distance float vague tree islands, and I know that houses hide there. Incessant winds bitch-slap those homes. There, pale Lutheran farmers huddle and shiver on this land they have killed. I don't know what they're doing. They may be in the wrong bedroom ogling their daughters, or they could be at the kitchen table estimating the number of corn kernels in the total harvests of their ancestors. It does not matter. The only natives who survive here are the crows who laugh and thrive and dive through the bitter air of their own appreciation. These crows are shadows of all my loved ones who've died by their own dark hands. I join their black chorus of curses against the coming green of springtime and against the poor farmer's folly of greed. I wish I could say I know better, but I'm a citizen of a dazed and defeated race. You may have seen me, sometimes indignant, sometimes indigent, and too often, when it suited me, indigenous.

THE RECONSTRUCTION

At a cocktail party after a reading in Wisconsin, an iceberg-breasted redhead from some leather planet asks if I've ever written "hard-core" porn. The glacial whiteness of her Caucasian flesh frightens and tongue-ties me. I mumble something I pray sounds professorial yet hip (as if "hip" were still hip) and then fade into the fetid sanctuary of poverty's memory. I hold my breath until I become perfectly invisible inside a tent of my inadequacies. Days later, back at my safe house in the evil Minnesota corn, I begin a novel of this neurotic, mammary night:

CHAPTER ONE:

My biceps are taut and bulge like they did at twenty-five, and I can still do the big-boner-boogie at the drop of a hat. I twitch smugly, stare deep into her green eyes and whisper: *Stretch your tongue out long. Make it into a whip—whip my plump ass good, whip me until I whine. Then elongate your pink tongue into a lasso. Cinch me up by the neck. Turn your pale arms and legs into wheels. Give your breasts a pickup grille. Take off, pulling me behind, dragging me bumpity-bump over the pavement until flesh dances from my bones and joy comes to the crows who blacken this dead nation's sun.*

THE CROW CHRONICLES

Raucous crow calling loudly from nowhere
only once means someone's lost.

— BRUCE WEIGL

False dawn brings an insomniac's electric mind and
endless cawing thoughts in flight. Snuggled in my
house, I smell manure-blanketed fields seeping through
my walls. *This is a bad-spirit place!* It's Thursday,
5:30 a.m. and I'm past fifty. A psychic pissing contest
of good and evil has interrupted my much-needed sleep
all night, and now Gerbit, my big nutless tomcat, has
hauled an overweight crow onto my frayed couch
where I'm courting the soundless television. Startled
into clarity by the headless bird, I find some old gloves
and drop the half-eaten creature into a plastic shopping
bag and then stagger through West Nile virus
mosquitoes to my '85 Crown Vic. I drive through the
lost empire of corn in the hazy daybreak of an early
Minnesota summer.

Unshaven, wearing a T-shirt, shorts and slippers, I'm
the only thing moving in this green morgue. I haven't
the foggiest notion of what I'm doing until I birth the
idea of dropping the bagful of avian pulp in front of the
Morlock County Sheriff's Department because a stark,
young Nazi gave me a speeding ticket last week. Like a
drive-by shooter, I toss the crow out the window at the
brick gendarme bunker and then weave back home, a
little excited and smiling to myself—another goofy

episode in the moronic movie of the graying, once macho poet. (But, oh how charming and professorial I was to the young Republican junkyard dog who wrote the ridiculous ticket in the first place!)

Back at the house, I find that Gerbit has puked a huge lump of bloody feathers onto the landlord's ancient carpet. I use paper towels to scoop it up, spray Windex on the spot to remove the blood, and flush the lump of ravenesque residue down the toilet. What next from my stupid cat? And Gerbit isn't even the real Gerbit. He's a replacement, a dead-ringer I got for Colleen when the original ran away or got poisoned—never mind, that's a whole different fable.

I'm wide awake and don't know what else to do but have breakfast. I drown a huge bowl of Cheerios in milk and sugar and turn on the TV. I say, "Good Morning America" to semi-serious Charlie Gibson and smiley-faced Diane Sawyer who's always tittering like Charlie's secretly goosing her. America, like these moronic morning media whores, *is* the constant search for something to believe in and then forget, *like* the great democratic expansion that rafted down rivers of slave and Indian blood and dropped the many-tongued and fearful settlers here onto these Great Plains. Outside my window, angry crows stare into my house and curse the television with me. We both know any sense of true history is dead in America. I toss my soggy

Cheerios out onto the gravel driveway, and soon the crows are calm, eating breakfast and chatting amiably.

They are simply biding their time.

One fine morning they'll launch a sneak attack on Gerbit and peck his pecker off. And then I'll have to ride off into the Minnesota dawn with a dead, dickless cat in a plastic bag. Smiling crows by the thousands will follow my car. Countrified bumpkins jogging on the outskirts of town will join the dark procession and moan in unison. If that wild dog God could escape from *their* prison of churches, he'd heal me with slobber this bountiful morning.

THANKSGIVING IN THE PROMISED LAND

Fetid new foes have arisen this month. The land surrounding my rented farmhouse stinks worse than hell's outhouse. From the north they've shoveled out the turkey Treblinkas and spread the pungent delight onto fields. From the south slurry tankers filled from pig-shit lagoons are spraying the dead black soil with the fecund perfume of Azathoth. I drive to Cottonwood to gas up the car. On the small town school windows, grammar school kids are still pasting generational clichés of construction paper pumpkins, buckle-hat pilgrims, and perfunctory redskins with soft and generous Christian hearts. Mind-warped by the stink, I adopt their illusions. I give thanks to my can opener and to Campbell's Soup. I bow to Philip Morris for my wheezing breath. Special thanks to the pills that keep me erect and to a palsied sobriety that keeps me from fearing the flag-festooned pig that we ride.

MINNESOTA TURKEY DAZE

I have been trying to decipher the corn and my place in it, but I am repressing my guilt over leaving the one I love. I now have most of the corn puzzle parts. I *do* know that the earliest version of maize was born in Mexico. Centuries before the white man came, it spread from those southern climes to all the tribes of the north. *Compadres*, I have eaten corn tortillas from Guadalajara to Fargo, North Dakota. The few tree-hugging friends I can tolerate tell me that monarch butterflies winter in Mexico. Then they swim or fly over the Rio Grande and are poisoned by gene-altered corn on these Great Plains, but dead bugs do not trouble my heart.

It's all so corny, this meditation on maize. On the other hand, I have seen the western half of America super-saturated by Mexicans the past thirty years or so. But what all the Mexicans are doing now in Morlock, Minnesota is a mystery until I ask a janitor at the College of the Corn. "So what's the deal with all these Mexicanos, Señor?" He shakes his weary head and stares at me like I'm truly stupid. "They work at the turkey packing plants, you dickhead. Exactly how retarded do you gotta be to become a college professor?"

There are only two sources of necessary knowledge at the College of the Corn—the secretaries and the janitors. You are mandated to crawl into their caves if you need answers. And all arcane questions *will* be answered: What is life, what's the real IQ of George W. Bush, or how the hell have I gotten this old? My guru janitor, who thinks all professors are dickheads, finally tells me that most of the Mexicanos working in Morlock are *illegals*. "You never heard of wetbacks and fake green cards?" he asks, adding that the area's plants ship their best birds to Butterball® and he knows. He used to work at one of these slime-holes and when I ask what they inject into the Butterballs® he rolls his eyes, scratches his graying mustache, and slyly whispers, "Butter—you dick-headed egghead."

An hour later, while passing my office, he relents and tells me about how the local turkey farms cut off the top beaks of birds so they won't peck each other to death in the pens. "Some-those damn turkeys stare up into rain and get so much water down their missing beaks they drown," he says and laughs. I don't know if he's brain-jerking me or not. "Gobble, gobble," he whispers and turkey-trots, dancing his broom down the hall, past the classroom where in twenty minutes I will preach a sad sermon of grammar to fumbling freshmen who could easily be his children. At one time the woman I love would have easily understood all this, smiled enigmatically, and patted me on my bird-brained head.

ON THE COUCH OF NOVEMBER

Nescafé, the instant coffee is easier to make than fresh ground Starbuck's. The ease of any powder elevates the taste of life tremendously. Sunday morning, warming up the tube for a day of football, I stop on ABC, the figure skating network. I am hoping to see the spinning pretty boys bounce their butts on the ice. Ah, there is a God. As if on cue, nasty spills happen to three sequined skaters in a row. Some minor but extremely cruel hungers of middle age are easily appeased. Satisfied, I change channels to watch the spinning ugly boys bounce their monosyllabic butts on the plastic sod of sad Minneapolis.

ANONYMOUS DOGCATCHER HOTMAIL

Your wine-puke-purple Minnesota Vikings jacket envelopes your emptiness exceedingly well. But, I think if those ancient thugs actually wore purple then they were anachronistic fashion-plates, maybe even a little sexually ambiguous—Christ, okay I'm getting sidetracked. Yesterday you kidnapped my little, dying dog and held him for ransom. Right now I want to shove a light bulb up your rural backside and light you like you'd never been lit except for that drunken Republican morning when you swore Lady Liberty staggered into your bedroom and rode you to the raw and rising sun. I wish I could hold you down and let my little dog nip your nuts off and spit those tiny marbles out onto the cracked sidewalks of this blanched American town. But my heart is not that cruel, or I'd have signed my name to this note and set a date for a duel. Besides, my dog has no teeth left.

NAMING THE DANCE

Tonight is as dark as the anal desires of coffin worms. The pungent blackness of these moonless plains hoists all memory's anchors. Here, in the rural quiet of the northern Bible belt, the whispering cemetery across the road is not even faintly amusing. I turn on every light in this old house, but outside I hear hot, red blood burbling up from black soil, coating my ancient Ford. In the morning a big, four-wheeled scab is sitting in my driveway, pulsing in the bright air where the dry corn sways. In the morning, my body is covered with hair and wings have sprouted from my shoulders. I've become one of those flying monkeys from the "Wizard of Oz." I shrug and do a sheepish little jig that I name my "monkey-fuck rain dance." I hear a distant chorus serenading me. The moist and petulant daughters of evangelical sodbusters are begging to hold my simian hand.

ARSE POETICA

I.

Escorted down an Ivy League college hallway by beaming graduate students, I was introduced to one of those simple pudding "language" poets one encounters in such places. He was a callow though tenured nerd of indeterminate sex. I could've squashed his soul like a bug, but an unasked for rush of kindness made me listen to him for a few minutes. When I stripped off the flying fur of his words, I discovered that he had no heart and thus his wail was only an aria for the lack of true love.

He was young and loved poetry. I was middle-aged and considered it a curse. We had absolutely nothing to hold hands about except for the fact he was Minnesota born and I worked in that immaculate toilet of a state. He said *Bly,* and I bit my tongue until it bled cheap, liberal blood. He said *McGrath,* and I knew that I must smoke away such breathless banality, so I coughed, pulled out a Marlboro, and briskly walked away. Were I his age, I would have prayed for someone to grab my tongue and make me bleat rainbows of wet-scented shimmer. Were he my age, he would have wept, scurried back into the nearest wordless cave, drawn horses on the walls, and waited ten thousand years to speak.

II.

For me, poetry *is* poverty. All my life I have lived day to day, paycheck to paycheck, poem to poem, no rhyme or reason. Many of my students have had grotesquely romantic notions of crap unto craft unto fame, but I've no idea what they *thought* or if they *thought* at all, and I lack energy to lie for them here. Too many were technological tadpoles addicted to cable TV and the computer, those gifts given by the Roswell aliens to subvert common sense, human compassion, and history. Thus, I did not recommend poetry to them. Nor did I recommend them to poetry. Let them eat corn, I thought. Let them fall under the spell of the dead white poets who dance and drum in the deep, goofy woods of the bloodless mind. Better yet, let them sweat for years at a job they despise, but a job that their education had guaranteed. Then that gaseous thing they call *poetry* would either die or transform to stallions of flame igniting the blinding snow of blank paper.

III.

There you stood, on the edge of your feather, expecting to fly . . . Historically, his taking of poems seemed in direct proportion to penile function. Once, he saw poems everywhere and plundered them at will, eating only their tongues and livers. In the greasy glow of his faceless mind, he seduced many a young love and then lost focus. In the years that passed, their skulls and carcasses littered his landscape and made little sense.

In his youth he had brain-sucked too many skulls that were not his to eat: three hundred at Wounded Knee, thirty-eight at Mankato, the four dead in Ohio . . . In middle age he became so ashamed of his trade that he dug a hole into the side of a small hill like he'd seen the farming invaders do. He grew gray and misshapen. Many hard winters he passed on a diet of remorse and guilt. His hunting rifle rusted and rotted beyond recognition. His flaccid pecker refused to acknowledge the love of his own tender hand. Centuries passed.

Now, he sees an occasional poem ghosting through the mists of dawn, but he holds his breath, and lets it pass in peace. It's better that way. Anything spawned by the adulation of romantic losers, by the memory of memories, is better left unborn.

IV.

"Know this now, you are killing a man."

—ERNESTO "CHE" GUEVARA

You could call it grabbing the bull by the horns if you were ironic. No trumpets, no picadors, no banderillas. No muleta, no cape or sweet-stinking sinking of shining saber. The bull merely sashays into the arena, snorts the foul human air, and at the instant his eyes meet mine, I empty the clip of my .45 into his forlorn skull. Filet mignon or fecal-scented tripe, it all tastes the same in the unwashed dark. Oh *pinche gringos*—continue to plow the fields of the earth. Bury the shadows of anything tribal in the furrows. It's what you pray for. Jesus, it's what we pray for too.

V.

SMALL PRINT AT THE BOTTOM OF A CREATIVE WRITING SYLLABUS: Tell the truth, always tell the truth. Listen. Even though this is Christian Middle America, I know you've all dislodged a green booger, rolled it in your fingers and admired it. It was and is a beautifully ugly poem—the sad world in miniature—but if such wisdom seems beyond you, I hereby give you permission to hide those invisible snot-balls between the pages of the book you'll never have the groin to write. Don't look so sad, I've already written it for you. And of course, you'll all pass this course. So bless me, and bless me doubly in your course evaluations! They are only read, if read at all, by those self-gilded and transitory automatons we call administrators. But, should you pass my house late at night, bring the sweet and greasy marrow of your bones to the horndog corpse that I was and maybe will be again.

VI.

My increasingly fat cat Gerbit is on the windowsill chattering his teeth at a neurotic, brown dove preening on the front lawn. At the same instant, in North Africa (on the Discovery Channel) a caracal lynx is fighting with a black eagle. Oh, the zany Zen of it all, this skewed duplication upon my weary eyes. Outside the sun is setting and all I say, have ever said, is covered with the soft sauce of confession, my mundane madness of tattling on the world and on myself. In desperate revolt I open the front door and the dove flies away. I turn off the tube, and my mind flies back in. I shiver and shake in grateful appreciation of such silence. I know it won't last long. I want to whisper of other sweet doves I've shot with a .410, how I softly plucked and gently fried their sad-singing flesh. I want to tell you the story of how I was born to the bone-singing sun of the desert, but that tale is best left for the posse of clowns who will dismember me on my silk-sheeted deathbed.

VIII.

I suppose even a half-honest artist can create a true bonfire of vanities. With just the tiniest squirt of kerosene (and ten squirts of Jack Daniel's) I once watched a box of my books blaze beautifully, illuminating the smirking, sweating face of God. Under the drunken South Dakota stars I was thinking that the fact I graduated from an Ivy League writing program did not really make me a poet. I was thinking that the fact that some idiots thought my poems were delicious fruits and published books of my syllabic jism still did not make me a poet. For Christ's sake or ache, there are only a handful of real poets in this country, I reasoned, and they keep a low, skulking criminal profile. And sometimes they secretly burned their own books. I was thinking all this silly crap one night when the true love of my life locked me outside to contemplate my firewater epiphanies. And now, nearly sixteen years later, I pray that I can maintain my present irony, this sad exaggeration of the importance of poetry. I need to keep those paychecks rolling in while I thrash and shudder in true fear of the oily Republican darkness.

WISCONSIN

Mid-winter, physically sick of seeing corn stubble on the face of frozen fields and glad to be going anywhere, I let the airport Gestapo sniff my sneakers and flew out of Sioux Falls carrying poems to read in New York. At the reception that followed, an old friend, a muscular Black writer of note, swaggered up to me and I congratulated him on his recent good ink in the *New York Times Book Review* and he said, "It's sad as shit we think that rag's some fucking Holy Grail!" Momentarily taken aback, I finally asked if what he said was a poem. "Possibly, but leave my name out of it," he said, and I did. I do. So, my man, this brother ain't you. And I ain't me. This ain't a poem. It's just an aching, sidebar to an old man's jet plane pee. On the flight back home I stood up and wobbled to the restroom. Walking back to my seat, I chanced to glance out at the snow-covered mid-west. Small towns seemed nothing more than the blue mold on blue cheese. Treeless hills appeared and rose up like clumps of bland cottage cheese. Lakes looked like the holes in Swiss cheese. Somewhere down there on the frozen tundra, the Packers were breaking the hearts of cheese-heads.

E-MAIL TO WOODY

Hey Woody, I guess you heard Jim Welch is dead? Anyways, I assume you got weary of nibbling those down-home muffins on the soil of St. Ignatius and went back home to Siksika land. Tonight I'm thinking about that double trouble of NDN womanhood. My man, I am crazed and lonely in loony Minnesota. Tonight my heart is slow and black, blacker than your Blackfeet heart. And as we creep a few years past the millennium, I'm wondering if you're still thrashing away to those ancient songs of the sixties? I mean if you're still pumping to "Purple Haze" then you're a better man than me. You know damn well what I'm saying. We're entering the age of rare wood, yet we're still sadly gutpunched by fake-warrior passions like cooz and booze . . . It's so hard to choose, and at this age we got nothing to lose. With a fifth of Jack Daniel's and a suitcase of old ribbon shirts, I could blaze over to Browning and together we could bitch-slap those young punks who used to be us. But tonight *is not* a good day to die. And I'm too weary to discuss what waits for us up there in that cold, white sky. You get the time, drop me a line. I need some real redskin horseshit to blast out these corncobs they've jammed in my ears.

ME AND SIMON SEND SMOKE SIGNALS ON THE GREAT AND GASEOUS INTERNET

ME.

"Hey dog, I know you don't want to hear this, but I had a dream you were in the other night. Yeah, I know it's weird. I dreamed that you and I were sitting in a bar and you were trying to get me to drink and I kept saying no, and finally I started drinking and got shit-faced. Then we staggered down this dirt road to an old run-down motel, a puke-smelling dump like I stayed in on the outskirts of downtown Gallup one week many moons ago. We walked into the motel room and visible from the doorway was the bathroom. The tub was full of water and there was a young Indian girl, maybe 15 or 16 totally submerged in the water—dead, and we both ran away from there like chicken-shit drunks. I woke up shivering. That's about all I can now recall of the dream, but it was very strange and kinda scary. I don't know what it means, cuz."

SIMON.

"Yeah, that's strange and scary. Such dreams, such stuff scares the shit out of me. And you hear and see shit like that in and around Gallup, Holbrook, Albuquerque, Vancouver, Rapid City, and Phoenix. Hellholes our land has turned into. I used to be afraid, and still am I guess, to go into Gallup. Now I just pass by fast on the Interstate and don't look back. Well, look in the rear and side mirrors for the cops! Years ago once walking with a Navajo-Ute guy through a dark and dangerous-looking parking lot outside Milan's, a dive northside bar across "the Purky," we stumbled upon a guy with a knife stuck in him. Oh shit, what we gonna do? What am I gonna do? You don't know what the fuck to do, you just walk away fast muttering, cussing, and checking all the dark spots around you. Shit, man, you don't why, how, what, or nothing, a kind of panic you can't just push aside, no way. You get kind of brainless too. Sometimes I think you just end up cussing yourself for walking that way, being there, just being there, you blame yourself, in other words, you know, like it was your fault for crissakes, cussing yourself and the guy with the knife in him, cussing and blaming yourselves for being Indian, geesus."

GOD'S BEARD IS CAKED WITH CAMPBELL'S CHUNKY CHICKEN SOUP

When I'm driving to visit Bill Holm in Minneota, MN, Heaven dances into focus. Even with my flaccid arm, I could stand in the doorway of the high school here and one-hop a hardball down the street and into the nursing home. The question is—would I be there to catch it, or would I evaporate into a sarcastic angel while rounding the bases? Even God, the great umpire of the unimportant, is wary of making that call. He can never tell us the difference between entering Heaven and entering the home for faltering ancients. God, for Chrissakes, is senile too. His white beard is caked with Campbell's Chunky Chicken Soup. He squats like a catcher on his golden throne and stares into the mirrored mist of eternity, puzzled as he pounds his once-pert pudendum. Outside of town five hundred of his patrons, dull and arid farmers who could care less about the national pastime, pray for just one thick-clotted ounce of his miraculous moisture. These desiccated souls see Heaven as the wet spot they'll gladly lie in.

A TEMPORAL FELINE DISTRACTION TAKES ITS CLAWS TO THE CALENDAR

FALL.

It's been seven years or more since my cuddly kitten vanished and now, *now* another appears at my farmhouse door. She's wild with hungry loneliness. At first she doesn't seem cuddly at all, but I guess I'm affectionate enough for the two of us. I suppose she'll need shots for rabies and feline distemper. And I'll have to teach her how to transcend disappointment when I slip and moan the name of my other kitten who's gone. Lord, please make her understand that I do have other responsibilities, darkly jealous fetishes, and the clawing, unrelenting ghost of another kitten. *Don't let it bring you down; it's only castles burning.*

WINTER.

Muscular, tawny kitten. You come to me in my swirl of dry-land dreams, and I am amazed by your kindness, your desire, and your tongue that speaks your ancient language. You have the face of your race and in the mirror of your flint eyes, I see the man-child I was. You will take me away, down the road that leaves these prairies and up to the piñon-covered hills of my mythic labyrinth of desire. There I will bathe in the paradox of being young and wise at the same time. In tonight's sky, the crescent moon withdraws slowly after piercing the plump clouds and scared stars spritz in brief array.

The rains are coming, the rains and rebirth, my sweet little pussy.

SPRING.

I believe you're a kitten of witches. You are the bringer of dreams. For years I've asked for the spell to be cast and now you are here. Now this house elongates erotically. We slide down endless tunnels, through compound fenestration of room unto room, past windows of ever-changing vistas. You drag this middle-aged man through the wake of your juices, make dry bones dance awake to wet, almost forgotten songs, and I love you as I love the harsh desert blood of my ancestors. *E nu mu du wi.*

SUMMER.

O tawny flex of flesh and fluid. Bright eyes. Warm, brown arms. You are the bone and juice of all my desires. The hopes and fears of all my years are met in you tonight. Sweet kitten, I'm lost in the smoke scent of your black un-American hair. The ancient and still lush "After the Gold Rush" is on the sound machine and you're feeding me burnt toast and black coffee. Strong, lithe, and naive, you seem to be a delicious dream, but you *are* real, and I damn sure will not burst the bubble by asking how long you'll stay in this ice-country dream. Soft-black-furred kitten, if I have forgotten what love is, then I hereby rain anew the intricate wetness of that word with you.

ANOTHER DAY IN THE ENGLISH DEPT.
OR MEET ME AT MEDICINE TAIL COULEE

Let Bacchus' sons be not dismayed
But join with me each jovial blade
Come, drink and sing and lend your aid
To help me with the chorus.
(From *GARRY OWEN*, unofficial
marching song of Custer's 7th.)

There's this supremely blond kid from Fargo, North
Dakota in class who tells my two Indian students that
their poems whine too much! I'm just going through
the motions of metaphor and rhyme, but when he says
that, I twitch and wonder if an iceberg of Haight Street
acid has broken loose from some ancient mooring and
is now coursing my veins. I secretly pinch my thigh
and remind myself that I am indeed in Morlock,
Minnesota. Then the white kid says, "You Indians
should be thankful you weren't all massacred." Damn!
This (Stick a needle in my eye!) is what he says: "You
Indians should be thankful you weren't all massacred!"
I'm breathless because he's not using one iota of irony.
I call a ten-minute recess and retreat to the nearest exit
to smoke a smoke . . .

If this were a poem, I could contrive some witty
comeuppance where at the conclusion of this tale I slap
an ounce of sense into the junior storm trooper. An
ending where truth and justice triumphs is so
immaculately American, but my life is not a poem, and

this is only a brief bookmark in the trudging tale of a
middle-aged half-breed.

After class, I'm filled with guilt, shame, and impotence,
so I take the young *Dakotapi* out and buy them some
Grain Belt beers at the Legion bar. There is silence until
the third round arrives. Then I shake my head and tell
them that this is a very strange and screwed-up *wasicu*
town. They say, "Ayyyy." I tell them I am sorry that
they had to endure this, but they know I know they
know and all the rest of this horseshit nation knows:
*The white man is still in deep psychic turmoil for
stealing our land and calling themselves Christians at
the same time.* They nod their heads and drink. One of
the young Skins says, "Hey, we *should* be thankful we
weren't . . . all massacred!" and we howl deep NDN
laughs and ignore the golden poison glazing on our
souls. We drink and talk until closing time when the
full moon night brightens our once-dying eyes.

for Steve Pacheco

INDIAN WOMAN POPCORN PRAYER

Exhausted from teaching and too old and lazy drive unnecessary ice-roads to the market, I came home to a supper of microwave popcorn. Before collapsing to sleep, I prayed for a bright and shining, computer literate Indian woman to firmly grasp my vivid groin and dance me past the electrical poem of these daffy, new Dark Ages. Upon her arrival, I'd beg her to cage me in a microwave and pop the whiteness from of my soul. I'd implore her to make me light-headed and sappy, soaked in the rich butter of brilliant, tribal love.

I don't think I was asking for too much . . . but the next morning I awoke alone with a parched mouth and morbid loneliness. Winter had become summer. Outside in the bright morning heat, snickering fields of pregnant corn chided me for not using restraint befitting my age. I stood in front of my full-length mirror and did a brief war dance, lamely shaming the unmitigated gall of the mutant corn, the latest foil for all my foibles. Any Indian woman seeing that dance would make sure to stay dark galaxies away.

HIGH PLAINS BERMUDA TRIANGLE

Colleen, the best I can do now is sing dust songs like parched farmers praying for summer rain. The only fluid I possess is ectoplasm, a demon jism: a blend of spirit fluid and boozy flux. The two large fans in lieu of the broken air-conditioner cannot still dirty millers in their circumnavigation of a dim, bare bulb that flickers inside my hot head. The left fan is running a little faster than the right, but that doesn't bother me or my nameless co-pilot who has twisted open a fat, plastic bottle of Coca-Cola and is spiking it with an ample splash of charcoal-filtered Jack Daniel's.

Tender darling, I tell you I don't know this co-pilot. Does he look familiar to you? Shit, I hope that I'm not being abducted by aliens. He might have said his first name is Bill . . . Christ, I pray he's not one of those twelve-stepping Bills—or one of the shivering re-born, or worse, one of those butt-shaking, holy-rolling snake wranglers. Whatever he is, for sure he's a Skin.

"Between here and Borneo," Bill says, "are a hundred little islands that could support the good, red road as my great-great grandfather's children knew it." *There's nothing worse than a philosophical Indian.* I shake my head and dream my whiskey deep and straight. With each gulp my joystick grows larger. I'm entitled to such lies after a dozen years of being a dry drunk.

Down to one engine, our drab-green B-25 Mitchell is sputtering over Nebraska. Near the border of South Dakota and Huskerland, I spy a small man sitting in a small town. He's on his couch, sipping coffee. The problem is . . . his couch and the furniture he and his wife saved for is stacked inside a rental storage unit. What an odd sight. Oh, what a virulent, onion-eyed vision. I yell down to him and ask what it all means. "My wife passed away," he shouts. "So I come here every day to have coffee. It's too lonely at that rusty nursing home prison. Those goddamned people are dying there. Jesus, don't you think they'd know better?" I nod knowingly and wink as we zoom past his thick-tin shed deathbed.

The sky becomes neurotic with lightning. Sky-sparkle feeds on itself. No doubt such electrical madness totally vaporized any purported B-25—evaporated any vision of a drab green Mitchell with Betty Grable on the fuselage. My cell phone is crackling and my incessant loneliness is cracking. *Well hello, Mr. Soul . . .*

Some god-awful, lonely voice is cackling fifty miles south from her cramped, low-income housing. "Come on down," she says with the ever so slight hint of her parents' Sinaloa. "My legs want to squeeze you hard," she purrs and softly giggles above the crying of *dos* dark-skinned babies on her living room rug. Then she moans explicitly into the buzzing telephone. *I'm too old for this coronary potentiality.* "Lucita, we could get electrocuted," I say and pray we will. "Let me call you back after this storm passes," I plead. "*Guapo*, I feel really nasty tonight," she yells in pure truth like someone who's lived long past twenty, though she has not. The phone goes dead. I look up into the night sky and see the brown-skinned face of the only God I have ever known.

I reach for my keys.

I enter the storm.

BREAKDOWN BOOGIE DREAMS

DREAM ONE.

Home, after a lame party that predictably descended into a sad, slurred chorus of unscholarly state college professors bemoaning the transitory and blatantly false energy of administrators, I eat a Subway sub and then sleep and wake and sleep and then wake.

Late this manic night FOX news comes on and says Mariah Carey's been hospitalized with some sort of nervous, ejaculatory breakdown. Half impressed, I *do* wonder what chemicals she's been doing recently. I scan the channels and see her latest video on mindless MTV. She's warbling nonsensical vocables—from-the-hood-style with no lyrical substance. They say she's sold more records than any other woman in history. But her incessant inclination to bend and burnish every single note is irksome, even for an ever-juicy-lioness, groin-bump-grinding like those drooling fools in her imagined audience are bidding bloodstone diamonds for her flesh.

Mariah looks white, but she says her dad was a black cat. If so, she got short-changed in the Department of Soul. She's got a huge voice, but she can't sing. Despite her delicious body, she's archetypal, American idiot food. And now she's being publicly schizoid, but maybe I can help her. Yes, let me help you, Mariah darling, let me be your cornfield Minnesota pimp

64

daddy. *Oh, Mariah, drive your bi-polar Mercedes over here to these high plains. Come on down to entrepreneurial Morlock! We can break dance, break down, talk nasty and roll together in the rasping, evil corn. Then in the morning I'll cruise into my professorial parking place with your thong hanging from my Ford's antenna. Male students will throng, whip out their dreams and pray. Oh Mariah, damn-oh-damn this whacked-out American anthill you and I woke up to swarm out of.*

DREAM TWO.

Later the same week . . . Sweet fornicating dreams redux! I'm doing the twist (how original!) at the Peppermint Lounge in Reno, NV. It's September 1966 and I'm wearing a black suit, a thin, luminescent green clip-on tie, and suede "fruit boots." I have a Beatles haircut. The girl I'm dancing with is sweating stinky and has hair starched to stone from hairspray. I pray that I'll be able to get into her high-waist panties, but then I am young, rural, and as dumb as my purple-headed yogurt slinger. And just *what* am I doing in a suit and tie at eighteen besides attending my own funeral?

HOG HEAVEN: A PORCINE EPISTLE

for David Lee

Lord, guide me to drink only decaf at dusk. All night long I've tossed and turned aside a dream of meeting *El Diablo* in a cornfield where he tongued my ear with sordid tales of his huge and scabrous tool. He wanted desperately to notch me, but I can't recall his face or if he had horns. I distinctly remember no mention of money for my puny, half-breed soul.

I awakened unto snow. Disembodied, I trudged into dawn and shoveled the ancient sidewalk. As I swept the car, I saw a huge hog standing silently in two feet of sludge. Its ugly snout was icy. Its greasy, electric eyes met mine and dined. I don't know why the filthy beast was loitering in my lonely yard. Frozen drool hung from its jowls. *What the hell are you doing here, you ugly devil,* I whispered. I backed away slowly and went in and grabbed my pistol and smokes and came back out to face high noon. *Do not forsake me, oh my darling.* (Gary Cooper, you seemed so NDN!)

Don't be so melodramatic, man, the pig said and snort-farted. *And if you're gonna shoot, go ahead, make my day and do the fucking deed. You'd be doing me a big favor. It's colder than the dingleberries on a Duluth dachshund out here.* I took two steps backwards to clear my head and assessed the situation. *Listen piglet,*

I don't want to shoot you, but you are trespassing. I may not be the legal owner of this farm, but I am renting this dump, so go home, go back to the stewards of the land . . . your farmers, the very spreaders of pigshit. I'm gonna count to ten.

The pig cleared its throat and spat. *You call the farmers my friends? You're not as dumb as you look, are you? You know damn well that first they killed the Indians and then they killed the land itself. Come on, you watch TV and must know how they're always whimpering in public about "saving the family farm" and whining about corporate greed when in fact they are the corporation. What I say is—now is the time for all good pigs to come to the aid of the pork nation. Oh farmers, now is the time to take out your family shotguns and unburden us taxpayers!*

Now that was a truly fine pig speech and I have to admit he almost had me. For a long time I was nodding my head in agreement, but then he made a fatal mistake that sealed his doom. *No way in hell do pigs pay taxes!* I released the safety on my hockshop army-issue .45 and aimed between its eyes. This land does truly reek of pig shit, and it's driven me mad. It's not only the factory farms, but also the owner-operated cornfields that stink of pig. Some white farmers claim that this stench is "the smell of money," but there's no way in God's hell that greasy pork is "the new white meat" even though they've actually transplanted a pig heart into a white man. And how many American Indian hearts have been stilled by pig fat? And—footballs are not pigskin! They come from a friggin' cow. Actually one cowhide can make twenty NFL footballs. And one cow soul has got to equal twenty pig spirits. So, pork the pig farmers. *And pork you Mr. Pig. Or should I say, "My Lord of Darkness"?*

And then the pig oinked. *Wait, wait, wait! I swear upon the vertigo of the Virgin Mary that I am not the devil. I vow I'm a pure Lutheran porker. Besides, I can grant you three wishes.* The pig smiled and shuddered. I was shocked to see lard shiver in the bitter cold and a hot hint of pity swept through me.

Three wishes? Well, this half-breed has never been one to look a gift pig in the mouth. I'd glom onto two desires and then wish for three more wishes!

Okay compadre, I said. *Don't tell me no tales of Circe, but do come on in—have some of this good Mr. Coffee coffee. I'll whip up some store-bought eggs . . . and fry up some relatively lean bacon—if you don't mind.*

GAUDEAMUS IGITUR

Under April sun, monosyllabic farmers, cooped up all winter, roar tractors into fields that are too wet to be plowed. The blacktops are soon covered with mud. After I drive to school, I find my car is as muddy as a feedlot hog. Inside the College of the Corn, worried professors are filling their Professional Development Plans with fluffy, feel-good fabrications. Outside, even the clatter of spring football practice is disheartening. New cleats chewing up the green foretell yet another losing season. On the small and recently non-smoking quadrangle, a frail Malaysian student in a wheelchair feeds popcorn to greedy blue jays. On the right shoulder of his black shirt is an epaulette of white bird shit. The Zen of futility is unbearable and lovely and everywhere I look. *Gaudeamus Igitur.*

GRAMMATICAL NEANDERTHAL

In the Great Basin of tenuous memory, a skinned rabbit above smoldering sagebrush branches on dry, desert soil was the smell of God. Then THEY came. In the written history of *their* beginning, the word was *theirs* and *their* word multiplied crazily. Thus *rock* became *hand* and *hold* and in the same mouthful *smash the craniums of the natives until they can make no historical sounds.*

We knew how to fight for our food, for our families, but we knew no religion of widespread destruction and murder. Although we couldn't spell it, we sensed, and then feared the meaning of *their* survival. My grandmother's parents were born before they made our land a state, a star in their flag. So she knew firsthand we *were* different before they came. *Taibo ain't no good,* she said to her peculiar, little green-eyed grandson.

SURVIVAL. Survival is such a strange word for loving life. For most of my life, I have pissed my pants before inferior others simply to keep a paycheck rolling in. Of course this is the core of capitalism but here is the truth of any tribal vision. For the buckskin-thonged savages dancing in the flame-licked caves of night there dwelt no guilt. The breath of tomorrow was the bedtime prayer. *Grandfather, let us have meat and warmth and loving care for each other. Let the sun dance on the darkness of our shining families. We are and always will be our own loving redemption.*

SURVIVAL. Now we live in a world of strangers, made more alien, more apart from each other by computers, television, and Republican fundamentalism. Trapped in my final profession, I now stagger from windowless cave to cave wondering how is it these kids have made it to college lacking what I learned in junior high English. I don't know how many times I've said: "When a dependent clause begins a sentence, it has to be set off by a comma" or "A sentence is a complete thought, a group of words with a subject and verb." This is the poetry they pay me for. I can no longer comprehend or even hum any true songs of freedom.

I have been sentenced to institutional slavery. I get summers off for good behavior. My grandmother would be proud as hell. I'm the first in my family to ever gravitate to and graduate from college although my mother did make it through the Indian Nursing School in Window Rock, Arizona in the early 1940's.

And so, as a matter of survival, I continue to say that a comma is "a pause, a breath." *A breath that verges on breakdown, not quite a coma, but still a downer. Regardless of how I break it down, it's a paycheck. A rock in the hand. A smash to the cranium. I do what it takes to strut through the terrifying shadows of this pale world I'm glued to.*

ZOLOFT

I tell my doctor that *of course* I have constant dreams of Goggles and our years together with Colleen. Then, joking, I say *of course* I have constant dreams of Colleen and our years together with Goggles. He forces a nod at my lame joke. My life is filled with mundane chaos and sharp, flesh-stabbing sadness. It's as pitifully poetic as it sounds. Because he's an INDIAN HEALTH SERVICE doctor, he wants to give me a pill. I tell him I've already taken the largest pill there ever was. I've swallowed the earth and soon will vomit it directly into the sun. Then the white-bright boys and girls of this greedy, Christian nation will have only seconds to shudder and pee their panties before the final Ghost Dance songs are sung. The doctor just shakes his head and laughs. I like him. He takes good care of me. In '68 I would have snapped up his offer of free drugs in an instant and freak-danced down the psychedelic streets on my perpetual hard-on.

FOR AN INDIAN GIRL I ONCE KNEW IN MY STONE-SHADED AND TUMESCENT PAST

Sometimes you know me. Sometimes you don't. It's only been two weeks since I've seen you, but it seems like many moons. We make brief eye contact and shimmer like cold stones sprung from frozen fields. After more than two years of silence, you say "I love you," and then you lapse back into utter wordlessness. You are not facing me when you say these words. You're pacing the circular walk in the patio outside the Alzheimer's unit. Where do these words come from? Are they meant for me? Am I hearing voices? The orb of spring braises our hearts, but historical trauma still scents our hair. Who understands the ragged dance we do? Our rock and roll is not quite new. Years ago I would tease you and say, "Let's go in the bushes and screw." Now, finally, we may be too old. Just give me your trembling hand to hold. Look there, the mute lilacs are budding. The lilacs darling, and my eternal blue love for you.

A MONTH AFTER NO E-MAILS, I CALL BACK EAST AND LEARN YOU'RE DEAD

Oh goodbye softly sweet one, it was splendid while it ran.
Goodbye my bitter, white girl—I'll forget you if I can.

—PETER LA FARGE

Jeanne, you said you supposed man made art because
we have poor memories and constantly forget what
beauty is. I said we have art because God, in his
infinite madness, planted death and loss as the
backbone of man's hobbling existence. Maybe we were
both right. Kid, you split quicker than a broke bum
from this cheap, old hotel. Exploded aorta. Fast and
sweet. No lingering rebellion of tired flesh. No sad and
endless decay. And because I live on a different planet
than I did in '72, I didn't find out about your death until
a full month after your cremation. Jeanne, I know it's
middle-aged lunacy, but I can't help but wonder if
white smoke drifted up from your bones. Goddamn it, I
distinctly remember when we met on a green wooden
bench in the Boston Commons and smoked a thick joint
of righteous Panama Red and how you followed me
home to the Back Bay dump I was living in, how we
seriously! discussed H. P. Lovecraft, how we screwed
and giggled with Tim Hardin on the stereo, and how we
then spent eight years of living together in the
backwoods of Providence, crazy and high and low, low
like I am now. Sweet Jeanne, I just got the phone call
about your death fifteen, nut-numbing minutes ago.

Now I'm listening to a Townes Van Zandt CD, and I want to drink hard, guzzle for now and forever the fragile eternity of our ancient innocence.

Jeanne Anne, sometimes, through the mystery of miracle, vision is restored to people who have been blind all their lives. But what if their first sight is a hell filled with semen-spitting snakes and straight-razor wielding clowns who seek to blind them again?

Jeanne, sometimes my thoughts are crazed . . . I wish I could talk to you about my Colleen's Alzheimer's. The cliché they use is that the person suffering from it does not suffer as much as family members and caregivers, that it's really harder on the loved ones, but I have my doubts. Sometimes I think she has milliseconds of phosphorous clarity when she sees the overwhelming tragedy of this disease, the mindless horror of it all, and it makes her stagger for a moment, and then she keeps going, head down into the mental blizzard, and I don't notice, I don't notice. I don't notice! I don't . . .

Dear, dead Jeanne, do you know what I'm saying? I mean what's worse, body death or brain death? Or are they both beautiful? And if she arrives before I do, will you protect her until I get there? Will you please for Chrissakes watch over my woman?

PLAINS INDIAN RIDDLE: JUNE 25*th*

I get off the interstate at Mitchell, SD. The station wagon ahead of me in the drive-thru at McDonald's has DOC plates from the Boy's Reform School in Plankinton. There's a flabby, white middle-aged driver, and two Skins in the back, maybe fourteen. They appear to be twins. They're laughing, sweet smiling boys, swimming through the screaming fog with bright, blighted fish eyes. On the ridge above McDonald's, the west wind is keening, or maybe it's the ghost of Custer, still screaming for Benteen to come and perfume the wild shit smell of death's wet kiss.

CHRISTMAS PRESENT

Colleen Marie, I have your mahogany crucifix in this house of pine. And I have an irregular heartbeat that intoxicates me with hearty fear. My organs are besieged by doubt. A century after Henry Ford, deer still dance into headlights except for tonight when they clatter onto the roof of hope until my skull caves in. Late this night, unable to sleep, I eat one of the candy canes I bought for you in your nursing home. Seven long hours away, I can hear you whispering my name like the holy rosary. I taste the sweetness of the red and white stick and the sharp memories of our *iyeska* lives. *As it was in the beginning, is now, and ever shall be, world without end.* The only gift I offer this year is the tired cliché of my heart. Next year, my love, I promise, I'll do better. I promise . . .

METAPHORICAL MORLOCK, MINNESOTA

Bleak semis blast past midnight, making furious curtains of lacy snow. In their wake, dim streetlights give up the ghost of this small town like an unwanted computer pop-up. Beneath the stinking smoke of the ADM Corn Plant, Morlock is a sleepwalking farm girl seduced by technology and the Bible. Her bleached hair is piled high like women on the Holy Roller Network. Her double chin quivers from Prozac. She's clothed by K-Mart and fed by McDonald's. Tomorrow she'll squat in my night class unnoticed by all my students who know it all. I'll fake the deep fathoming of rhyme and meter, and forgive the misdemeanors of their miscreant minds until she seduces the clock and they're gone, headed to the shallow abyss of their homely beds. Then I'll take her hand, kiss it gently, and beg for the key to this prison's door.

A HERMIT IN A BLIZZARD

At dawn the fat, American snow glues itself to the highway. At noon, a perverted wind turns the pompous flakes to powder. A disoriented snowplow leaves the county road and gouges a swath on my gravel driveway. Hungry, little brown birds flock to the frozen, rubbed earth. Pigeons huddle near the corncribs until a lone crow chases them into the frozen, stinging void. I devise a plan to ration cigarettes. I've got plenty of dog and cat chow. I have a large sack of potatoes, a microwave, and a tub of sour cream. I have the good company of two heaven-blue automatics and the ambiguous whispers of angels.

DEER AT MY KITCHEN WINDOW

Sister! I saw your tracks earlier. I'm making Campbell's chicken noodle soup. Excuse my messy house, but I'm sick with a brilliant head cold again. So . . . have you come to cure me or kill me?

JAZZLY INCONSEQUENTIA

And so it comes to pass that a young and increasingly rebellious poet in the department says he can get my tired breath published in the *American Poetry Review!* Excuse the drum roll, I don't mean to be mean, but at my current state of decay I really don't need no stinkin' *American Poetry Review.* I appreciate the offer, but I'm too busy building a jazz combo out in my old, red barn. I've got no bass, no piano, no drums, but at least I can sing. Listen:

The sky's a sea of dark, cheap wine.
Killer mosquitoes are thick, thickity-dick thick.

Watch out the sting. The sting feels like church.
Sweet church of snake-licking Lutherans!

Blood, blood, Indian blood is the sky and
the fat corn is rising so furtively.

My lips are so blue, true boo-hoo-hoo.
It's true, it's true, so screw you-hoo!

Someone once told me a wiggly road leads straight to the song and man, oh man, this tune ain't easy. But, it's mine and I'm fine, really-truly, I am.

for Giuseppe

FATA MORGANA

In tonight's dream you come to me, unrequited love of 3rd grade through high school. You've matured only into the butterfly of your 20s, but I'm still this plump, bulldog of middle age. You pat me on the head like one would pat a fat, old mutt and I grovel at your pert, white feet. Then you sit on me like I was a lawn chair! We become entangled so very wetly, smooching, talking that 60's jive. I awake feeling good for the first time in the many molasses weeks of ugly, high plains springtime. I rise from my couch, wipe the sleep from my eyes, and fry five eggs. *Two for you and two for me. And one for the half-breed boy who lived down the lane.*

ANOTHER DEER AT MY KITCHEN WINDOW

Sister! I saw your tracks earlier. I'm making nuked potatoes with *I Can't Believe It's Not Butter.* Excuse my messy house, but I'm half a century old and stressed to the max. So . . . have you come to tease me or give me a righteous beastfuck?

EXPLAINING MY EERIE SCREAM TO
THE NERVOUS STRANGER IN MY BED

When I was twenty (in the time warp of northern
Nevada) a tick tacked onto me. Oh, I was beautifully
young and incredibly quick-strong. I'd kicked my own
ass in Indian bars to the north and south of my home
soil, so I let it have its fill. Decades later when I finally
became a mature man, I saw that it had grown as big as
a watermelon off the wild juice of my veins. Then, when
I began to walk lopsided, I *knew* I wasn't getting jack
back from my kindness so I tried to yank the evil beast
off, but its head stuck in my flesh. It festered and
caused this *and* all my other screams. I'm sorry I woke
you sweet girl. No, no, please don't get up and go.
Here, drink this chilled glass of blood. Savor it, toast
my confusion, taste the dark prayers of my ancestors,
their thick, saline sacrament.

DISCARDED LINES FROM A LOST LIFE: THE 1964 HIGH SCHOOL YEARBOOK AND ITS SAD EMISSION OF GHOSTS

1. ROCK & ROLL

There was a boy. A strange enchanted boy, doing the twist in the high school gym. Look at those pegged Levi's. That flat-top! That Old Spice poverty! Oh, those flaming balls now cooled to stone.

2. LOCK & LOAD

I remember that fantastic TD catch Butch made when we were juniors. Three years and a short galaxy away, he crossed the goal line in some dank jungle and heard no cheering crowd. His name is on the black wall—the black wall in the black city. Sing a song of sixpence. Sing a song of sixth sense. Sing the blues with all these clues. Deep, dark, dank-people blues.

3. THINGS ARE ROUGH ALL OVER

God almighty, that thin boy with broad shoulders and gunboat arms is really me, photographed from the back. I remember that green brocade shirt, those penny loafers I bucked bales for. Under white Nevada sun, I tossed hundred pound bales as easily as sweat. That shabby guy I'm with is my best friend and that paper sack I'm carrying holds baloney sandwiches made with my mom's home-baked bread. They are neatly wrapped in wax paper. They are clearly wrapped in a love and responsibility it will take me a lifetime to learn. And what *is* bread but water and flour, yeast, oil, baking powder and love and responsibility?

I was always ashamed of home-hewn bread, the risen flag of the lower class. Behold the mixed-up, half-breed kid. That boy whose dirt-poor family never once ate together in a restaurant. Well maybe that one time in our pickup in front of a Mason Valley bar when Mom staggered out with big bags of greasy burgers and cold French fries for us kids in the bed of a pickup truck.

4. *NO LIE . . . HARDEE, HAR, HAR*
What Butch, my very best friend, said when I told him I had finger-banged the dark and beautiful fullblood René Marie Brown.

5. *I WAS YOU I'D THINK ABOUT THAT*
What her bug-eyed, greasy, Elvis-haired brother said when he found out what I'd said. "Hey ass-wipe, you think you're some kinda stud or something? I was you I'd really think about that." Then, looking down at his scarred Paiute fists, again he said, "No shit, I was you I'd think about that."

I was you I'd think about that?

I was you I'd think about that! Huh? In that confused instant my own fist is dancing against my own face in the bathroom mirror. In that exploding-star moment, I am dancing naked and crazy and I know I must be dreaming, but I'm cool, so cool that even the reawakened and ancient Indian-hating bluecoats who are standing over me and crooning cannot discern my intentions. I don't even know my own intentions except to delight in the brilliant stars swimming around me as I kiss the darkness.

6. *HERE'S A DIME, CALL SOMEONE WHO CARES*

What her mean, two hundred and fifty-five pound brother said when I said I was sorry, after he sucker-punched me in the nose and then kicked me in the nuts. He not only said, "Here's a dime," but also tossed a slim, silver coin down to my writhing soul.

7. *TAKE A PICTURE, IT LASTS LONGER*

What I said to my idiot friend Butch when he asked how I got the massive blood-smears on my shirt.

8. *MAKE LIKE A TREE AND LEAVE*

"Bite me. Why don't you make like a tree and leave," I said to Butch. "That's a laugh and a half," he snorted. I told him I wouldn't trust him as friggin' far as I could throw him. He giggled and asked who beat me up with an ugly stick. I told him to bend over and kiss his paleface ass good-bye. I was gonna kick his Caucasian butt. He said, "You really wanna fight over stinkfinger? Howzabout dry hump? Maybe third base? Who died and made you Queen For A Day? Knock yourself out then. I'll give you the first swing for free." I decked him good and he shouted, "What *is* your problem? A sucker punch like that don't show no hair." I shrugged. "You said to hit you. You fuckin' well deserved it for telling Rene's brother what I told you in secret."

"I'm sorry," he said, stuttering and half crying, and making me really feel like low-down crap.

"No sweat," I said, forcing a strange, fake smile. "Adios, shit-for-brains. Don't you ever talk to me no more. I mean it. Ever." And I walked away forever.

9. *CENTURIES LATER*

Reading his Butch's name on the shining black stone, I think I hear him whisper, "I'm sorry," until I realize it's my lips squeaking that useless American mantra.

"Adios, shit-for-brains," I gurgle and sprint from the shimmering silence of ancient history. Then, a block away, I decide to go back and get one of those rubbing sheets the Park Service gives out. I rub his name off the wall and carry it with me to the nearest DC saloon. I order a greasy cheeseburger and coffee, strong, brown, and bitter. At the bar, lower level government drones in suits are sipping whiskey and the amber medicine looks deliciously tempting.

BLUE HORSE

You say your valleys were so juice green that they were blue. With bullets flying and ancestor blood begging blue flies, you stood silent as ordered while women and children crouched down beneath fear-sweating foliage. Eventually, they became as green as their blue future in this sad, new world. Now, when I touch your flank and swallow your murmurs, I can taste the death rattle of each and every one of this carnivore planet's lost tribes. Oh blue horse, if the dying trees give us enough paper, we will ride over the powdered bones that constitute each and every scorched sugar mountain on this Aryan death star.

A SAVAGE AMONG KIDS OF THE KORN

In his lecture, the Indian professor recalled that famous foggy winter photo of the huge *Dakotapi* camp at Ft. Snelling and said it was a forerunner of Hitler's concentration camps, said it was the inspiration for Auschwitz et al.   And it all started *here* in Minnesota!

The white, bright, and beaming students choked on *his* truth for a second and then they tittered, many of them smirked, some left the lecture hall. I scratched my balls, scrunched down low in my seat, and watched the Indian wars rage on.

WITCH WIND

Slam me, sweet howling, ceaseless bitch of night. Bang me, my gritty, grindstone wind. Do me deadly, black wind of ash purity. Oh wind of divine and sober retribution, why do you try to break the barren trees and me? Why do you try to blow the souls from the cemetery across the road through my walls and into my mouth? I am not afraid, but I might not like the dust of their white words. I'd spit, but then you'd spit their withered tongues right back in my face. So, kill me, but spare me any dry taunts of Elysian Fields or Jehovah's stale, white bread Heaven. Give me a quick, dark and ancient death. Cold obsidian with no K-Y jelly, slid roughly into the heart like rabid Israeli bulldozers snarling unto tribal Palestine. Sand Creek plagiarized and mechanized.

LOGORRHEA

Facing surgery again, now six years after two drastic operations in which my colon was sliced and diced, I ask my beautiful doctor what the holy hell caused my original diverticular abscesses. *We don't really know,* she says. *Maybe a lack of fiber in the diet. So I hope you eat lots of vegetables, salads now?* I lie and say yes. I smile, wanting this woman who slashed my flesh to lick me like a lover. But salads? *Salads?* Potato salad, twelve times a year. Tuna salad, ten times a year. Egg salad maybe five times a year. In a blue moon, macaroni salad. Aside from those, I eat no salad except that stuff with canned fruit cocktail and Kool-whip. *Salads are my favorite,* she says. Through her veil of green eyes, I see her dancing naked in an ancient redwood forest. I know she's a liberal, but I *do* crave her knife again. I want the pure joy of my blood flowing free, the smirking face of God upon her scalpel and morphine, that sweet-flowing whore, deftly rimming my simple brain.

SISTER OF ST. FRANCIS

Winyan, I'm singing those bordertown blues again. Back home to our house of ghosts for the summer, I come across a crinkled photo of you in your ancient crow habit, smiling and strumming a six-string guitar. Regis College, late 60's, Denver . . . Bride of *wanikya!* Sister of St. Francis. Little Sioux nun from the flat lands of flat-lined South Dakota.

My love, now they say for the past two weeks you've been trying to choke your feeble fellow inmates and they want to increase your meds, and I say how can you choke when you only have one good hand, the other withered into a useless, dangling claw from Dupuytren's Contracture . . .

Take your good hand baby, make the sign of your wayward husband Jesus, sailing his wooden scaffold over a sea of blood-blanched, Indian nations. Colleen, I love you, will love you until I'm silent, and I honor your need to choke folks. I want you to choke me, choke me, darling into the airless equilibrium of your present Purgatory. It's okay. It's good. Airless, I can stroll down the ghost road until you breathe at my side.

A MEDITATION ON THE MEXICANOS IN SOUTHWEST MINNESOTA

From Quinchamalí where your eyes began
to the Frontera where your feet were made
for me, you are my dark familiar clay . . .

— PABLO NERUDA

My students look at me with mixed suspicion and awe when I scratch my chin and tell them that if the words in a poem do not explode into vision, the poem fails. There is nothing more insidious than an old artist telling his acolytes that he knows something truthful about the nothingness of verse. I have seen others do it without guilt, but I cannot. I might as well be telling them that the invisible piranhas of capitalism have already slithered up their legs and into their underwear. I might as well be teaching at forlorn Mankato State . . .

Explode into vision? God, how the years have dulled my sharp tongue. Growing up, we used to call the popcorn kernels that did not explode "old maids." Sometimes hunger forces us to chew dead ladies. I left my homelands at twenty and became a wanderer, but I've now lived in that dark and deadly window between the Badlands of South Dakota and the Sandhills of Nebraska for over twenty years. The years between my first 20 and the last 20 are a stoned blur. Now I've taken a job in Minnesota, seven hours due east of where my sweet Lakota woman waits for the cessation of mumbling agitation while she rides the howling roller coaster of dementia. I guess no matter where you go, it's the same old hat, but here in southern Minnesota nobody wears straw Stetsons except the Mexicanos, and they only wear them because they're piped directly *aqui de* Mexico and have prepared to enter some strangely dangerous western with Juan Wayne. Nobody seems to understand the Mexicanos, even though they're everywhere you look. I suppose they're mostly illegals, only one in a dozen seems able to speak *Ingles*. I do not know where they all live. I guess they work in the packing plants, but we use the same laundromat. That's okay because I would not be here unless *mi abuelo* Adrian Lopez y Mosqueda dogpaddled the Rio Bravo and stumbled up into the Paiute homelands of Nevada. But—hey, these Minnesota Mexicanos are very odd *Indios*. They're mesmerized by the washing machines. They stare in movie-theatre fascination at the spinning tale of detergent and their own fertile work clothes slashing water like *El Tiburón* in "JAWS." I pray for these Mexicanos and hope they will avoid the great white sharks circling now their sad, brown souls as they rise toward the lie of salvation, the lie of the Promised Land. *Compadres*, I welcome you. *¡Bienvenidos!* You *are* my dark and familiar clay.

JUNEAU INDIAN RIDDLE

In the Goldbelt beneath the "Spam Can," a girl of the Raven moiety said the magic words and I said they wouldn't work on someone as old as I was and that was so many lonely months ago now and I just wish I had shut my whining pie-hole and let her slowly rip my liver out with the shining black beak of her life.

SMALL TOWN VAMPIRES

In southern Minnesota I sure-as-shit have seen gray-haired vampires. Old vampires with wet groins and dry children with degrees from lazy state colleges. Late at night on small town streets, these gray-fangs join the parade of high school morons with soul shattering sub-woofers and cruise their caskets through McDonald's. Pallid when they should be plump and engorged, these ancient vampires whisper orders for blood-drenched burgers only to be stymied by cooking laws that forbid the eating of anything that reeks of the real. It's no wonder that recently hog farmers in the area have reported finding stock with fangs embedded in their thick, stinky hides. Now, when I look more closely at these rustic bloodsuckers, I see more than a few are wearing false teeth. I glance at their smiling wives seated next to them and nod. I too fear the cross, but with any quick snap of fingers, I would genuflect before the queer beauty of their enigmatic and smiling wives. I have never feared blood loss by bats . . . baseball bats, maybe, but neo-Nosferatus? Not in my lifetime of broken and gnarled knuckles.

IS THE ACE OF SPADES A RACE CARD?

Late in the spring semester and the processed food eaters in the classroom were getting restless, bored with word unto word, the rhetorical retreads, so I read them Etheridge Knight's poem about Tunji's talking drum which boomed *kah-doom-doom* and made all that had ever or would be said moot. The ensuing muteness of my students made me almost question my sanity so I slipped and said, "Now that's a poem that all white students should be forced to memorize." Then I glanced at the back of the class where a huge, black fullback was snoring in drum-darkened sleep. *Motherfucker.*

APROPOS OF APPROPRIATION, EXPROPRIATION, AND EXPIATION WITHIN THIS GREAT NATION

Despite your absent broomstick, I know you're simply a generic witch of the academy. Thus, when you saw the snail and the raven sleeping on the ground, you picked them up and put them in your pocket. Worse, you showed other people what you had found and said they were yours. When the snail and raven awoke and bit you on the ass, you expressed shock and outrage. Why is it that the obvious always eludes the blind?

Listen, dear plagiarist. We are here. And *you* are not. The words to our songs dance in *our* veins and in the blood of our blood. So don't tell us we are crimson when we're cerulean blue. Don't say we're cuddly when we're often cruel and pimpled with rusted spikes that skewer romantic pretense. My God, our breath is dead human flesh. We are here watching and we don't see you, your broomstick, or you're the black academic robes of futility.

In bleak lines you called verse, you pretended you knew us, and we wanted to scream and tell the world that you were simply a dilettante or a vampire, but we didn't. It wasn't necessary. We are here. You are not. We are ours to consume, cage, or kill. So stay inside the senility of your slant rhymes, don't venture outside the sanctuary of the tenured imagination. Hole up in those hallowed halls of fabrication. Go ahead, dab that sporadic, intellectual war paint on. We won't say a word about the circus, or about the pitifully perverted sex of academic clowns.

When we occasionally capture ourselves, never once do we mention your vampirical name, but under very intense self-interrogation we do say *yes*, we have met a few creatures like you, and when they stared at us with pens in hand, we simply shook our surly heads and howled like the last of our race. We're puzzled why our insane screams weren't frightening to the uninitiated like you. Our shrieking sent others of your ilk scurrying. Oh, *goofus academicus*, we're *so* weary of words. Just know we are caged in our own back yards. We are soaking our still-functioning groins in the metaphoric ether of ten thousand Washita Rivers. We still remember what it was like to shiver in winter's outhouse. We *can* free our minds to dance in the recollection of the smell of raw deer liver. And we *are* strengthened by the wild songs of brown, raven-haired girls. Indian girls. Wild Indian girls with talons tingling and eternally ready to slash.

A MISCELLANY OF NOW DEAD RED GIRLS

I.

Strange, how the snaking smoke of silver-green sage cupped in my hands and brought to bathe my body is like whiskey to a damaged liver. There is no healing here. No matter. Who the hell have I tainted except those I loved? Here in this land of square fields and square people, I fret over the subtle regression of hair. Darkness becomes light and then laughing darkness again. The purity of blood collapses against the ancient liquored memories of a mid-life man. I hereby surrender to the inevitable invocation of my own failures and the bitterness I've tasted. I have nothing but the Holy Bible of my printed name, my Willie Nelson and Johnny Cash CDs, and the succulent promise of springtime. There is a woman I love and I whisper her Indian name into the pungent prayer of rising smoke, but no one whispers back. Elysium, even in the living languages of two hundred or so North American tribes might be an illusion. Then again . . . I might have some old friends there.

II.

At a wine and cheese hoedown after I read poems at a college on the California coast, a lobster-red and clearly crustaceous full professor asked me if I knew a certain "Native-American-Indian" artist and I said no, even though I really did. Because I confess in my poems, perhaps he thought I'd do the same in talk . . .

Maybe it was her wild black eyes, sad and archaic as obsidian, that arrowed my lusting heart one night . . .
I'd always admired her work though her proclivity for switch-hitting made good and constant gossip. That never bothered me. There aren't many men in America who can't and don't fantasize the molasses of woman unto woman. Once, in that distant fog and for ancient reasons, she dragged me to her cave and removed the blue coat I had adopted. And that is all I will say except her hair smelled like the sweet-grass of her Manitoba. In fact, I didn't even say this. It's only the bardic echo of a withered ego bouncing like a basketball in the empty gym of my small town brain. But I can't just say, "Score one for the poet" and neatly chalk it up. In the end, the poet always betrays confidences. And in the end, the poet betrays himself by eating the dead flesh of past love.

III.

Distant thunder growls at the same instant my crazed intestines do. I'm cleansing my house with sage when you dance into my brain. Don't be confused that I'm now stationed in white-bread Minnesota. My darling, don't be bored by the constancy of my forked, blue tongue. I *still* recall that night of thunder at a Nebraska Indian conference. We stood in the stinging Lincoln rain and you let me lift your skirt and slide my desperation in. We were academic savages in a dark parking lot, twenty-odd years ago. Now you are dead and I'm a gray-haired ghost. Or maybe it's the obverse. But, woman, any time I ignite gray sage we can be green and pungent again. *Burn me, bright eyes. Burn me, sweet woman, with the soft brown memory of your fiery Oklahoma skin.*

IV.

In the Aryan Minnesota morning light, my old head buzzes like a horse fly. Sometime last night, the whipping tails of Achilles' horses clipped my wings and I tumbled down, unable to fly over the nightmares of my youth. My envy of their immortality made me court all the wet demons of my destruction. In this morning light, I cannot see horses, but the sharp scent of their sex lather lingers, sharp, but not as sharp as the memory of a dark-brown and now-dead girl from Kayenta, standing coke-stoned and lovely, next to me at Lucy's Tacos, West Washington, LA, 1982. We were having a jalapeño eating contest and kissing. We thought our ghost shirts would last forever.

CALLING THE CATS

22° below and no sign of my cats. Glass trees from the
recent ice storm sparkle blasphemously, fired by the
dim bulb of my porch light. I am descending the steps
to holy hell. Colleen is dying and so am I. I'm stupid
for standing out here with no coat, but the cats are all I
have to love. They were *her* cats. *Come back in, you
little bastards, before my balls fall off. (Like those
furtive fruits didn't flee eight winters ago!)*

HIS "HOLLYWOOD" FANTASIES PRODUCE A VISION OF DARING ESCAPE IN WHICH HE DISCOVERS GOD MIGHT EXIST

The "property" is going to be sold. No farm boy shenanigans here. Byzantine lethargy is broken free by the green, green light. This isn't Gatsby's green light. It ain't even an adjective or noun. It's an electronic verb form that's new to me. The LA white boys say the "property" got "green lighted." I know enough to say these words translate to something like "the check is in the mail." There's an instant vision of freedom, no more solemn students searching for wet paper bags to write their way out of. No more driving down fast-food boulevard to the red brick sanctuary of self-important snakes and occasional assassins of the soul. No more industrial farmland to ponder. I'll burp fare thee well to the cornball cornfolks! *I ain't gonna work on Maggie's farm no more!* With the greasy greening of springtime, Minnesota can kiss my half-breed ass good-bye. I'll glitter-dance west with my cats and last dog, my clunky old Ford, and my star-struck dreams.

MEANWHILE, BACK AT THE RANCH

I fall. I get up. *Shake it off, cowboy.* I fall. I get up. *Shake it off, cowboy.* I fall and refuse to get up. It's not like I'm in my cold coffin, but staring up at the springtime clouds, I envision a lone spirit winging skyward and quickly eschew the contrivance of sentimentality in any goddamn form. But, a *compadre* at the college says sentimentality is sometimes okay in small doses. OK. Simple statements work best with the cold calculations of mathematics. There is no other way to say it. Today Gizzard subtracted himself. The ancient baby boy is dead. *Man-oh-man-oh-man!* In the fart-harsh blue haze of springtime Gizzard goes. *Minnesota has murdered both of my dogs.* And if that weren't enough, on this day of Gizzard's demise, I learn that the sleazoid machinations of the tinsel-town types went haywire; the selling of my novel exploded into farcical nothingness and the short of it is that I'll have no other choice but to sign up for another dick-shrinking tour of duty at the College of the Corn. So—when leaves start to fall, look for me. I'll be strolling the campus professorially!

Man-oh-man-oh-man! There was an old poet who lived in a shoe. He had so many worries, he didn't know what to do. And the shoe, oh Christ, the shoe was beginning to stink like old men do.

IN THE BOSOM OF ABRAHAM

In the spring semester one of my students says (in Bible-bound ignorance) that the God of the Bible and the God of the Koran are two different Gods. Maybe that it not so preposterous as it sounds. I truly believe the Great Spirit who watches over the Indian people is not the evil, fearsome deity of the white man's Bible . . .

***

The Yellow Medicine River spawns fat and fearless possums that could bite my cat companions to raggedy bloomers of light. I hate looking to the Mount of Olives or King James, but Jesus, save my kittens from these cancer-ugly country rats. *Lord, kill these monsters and I'll be your sex slave.*

***

Then . . . the Lord, well, the Lord . . .
Goddamn it, the Lord ejaculates. A wondrous green-speckled day dawns and I regenerate (with palpable guilt) in the warm spring tumescence. I pack my car with dead books and animals and dirty clothes and hit the road toward the sanity that only arises for me once past the western shores of the Missouri River.

Before I can count the hours, I'm back at my little poor man's house in Cowturdville, Nebraska, eighteen miles south of Pine Ridge, SD, thank God, out of Minnesota and away from the nasty-ass possums. I've got the brain-killing TV tuned in to the Christian Broadcasting Network. Benny Hinn with his weird pompadour and middle-eastern accent is talking about angels and the first time he saw them—dude said he was asleep and a demon started to choke him and then the angel Michael saved his life! And I almost crap my pants when I hear this because last night I had a dream of being attacked by a hooded spirit, he was choking me and I woke up screaming. *This is the needle-eye truth!* No need for the fluff of purely poetic patter here.

***

A few weeks later I've cut my ass-length hair and I'm wearing an ill-fitting suit from the closet of my younger days. And, Hallelujah, I'm testifying at an evangelical prayer meeting in Potato Creek, SD and maybe my face is truly aglow with the Lordy Lord of Lords. Okay, this is not the truth. It's unforgivably make-believe. But who would know? This *is* America. Land of the free to be you and me! Land of eternal illusion and greed. Great nation of processed food eaters. But whatever our particular darkness, we all always fear that white God-thing when he sticks his hand into the greasy bag of popcorn people and snacks. Indian, Arab, Black man, or Asian--we all have feared the white man's God, but not as much as we've feared the white man.

THE LAST SHALL BE FIRST AND THE FIRST SHALL BE LAST OR SOMETHING SIMILAR

Some people have said the Bush administration is filled with Nazis! If so, the bush league bushido of these so-called new national socialists might make me want to drink a twelve pack of Heinekens and chant *Ho—Ho——Ho Chi Minh*, but then I couldn't or wouldn't recall the rest . . . Besides, who would remember? OK, Cheney, Rumsfeld, Ashcroft, and that mean-looking *Shaft* bitch do scare me, but I don't think they are Nazis. The Nazis wore spiffy uniforms. I do love those high-peaked caps, the blackness, the death heads, those iron crosses, the black garters, the black nylons, O Condoleezza, my love.

AURORA BOREALIS

At the computer, two in the morning, I'm trying to avoid the bloodless poem of the white-bearded, state college poet I refuse to become. My new puppy is upstairs with me, but she refuses to come into my small office. She's a border collie and typically neurotic, but something is amiss. She's been in here a hundred times before but now she whines and refuses to cross the doorway. Does she see a ghost? Am I dead and making her shiver or does she see the shadow people who occasionally besiege me? All I want is for her to jump on my lap and give me a quick kiss. She won't so I go downstairs and let her out into the July darkness. In the safety of the Nebraska night, I begin to shiver too. And what are those red and green curtains in the night sky but a legion of ghost relatives dancing behind a green stand of piñon?

SUN DANCE

For generations, most physicists believed there was nothing faster than light moving through a vacuum — a speed of 186,000 miles per second. But in an experiment in Princeton, NJ, physicists sent a pulse of laser light through cesium vapor so quickly that it left the chamber before it had even finished entering.

— ASSOCIATED PRESS

The sun rising over my insomniac eyes blinked so fast that it was night again. My soul was tender from retooling a hundred and thirteen episodes of my wayward and never-ending youth. This is no time for lies. I *am* one of those insecure horned-toads who made sure to notch his gun before he shot. From first to last, it was all the same. In the America I grew up in, we played that pecker-brained macho game. I broke the speed of light, but someone might as well have put a sack over the head of the nine-angled Universe.

Holy Mary, Mother of God. Pray for us sinners now in the hours of our dissolution.

There are many women I have loved, but there is only one woman I have loved with all my heart. I'm out on the Thunder Road of her reservation this bright yellow morning of her endless dying. A pain transcending poetry slaps my brain rigid. I unzip my skull and look for that sissy boy, Jesus. *Lord, Lord,* I yell like a man calling his best lame dog. *Christ, have you ever danced? Jesus, at the Last Supper did you ask the waiters about the true taste of woman? If not, my Savior, you must turn back the clock and reorder. Bring back Mary Magdalene for an encore. Let her whisper your name in the cedar-warmth of sweet, loving sin, in the beauty of laser-dancing light.*

Out past the foul outhouses, under the purple sky caressing the spring sage, there are Indian ponies that dance briefly at dawn. I walk among them smiling until a muscular buckskin mare kicks me in the chest. I writhe in the dirt as she canters away, far beyond the awakening light. A fat, black gelding shambles up to me. It is Babylon, the ancient horse of my youth. *Oh Babylon, how I've missed you. Let me grab your mane. Raise me from this stolen soil. I know it's too late to ride against the invaders and their mindless drool of technology, but just let me cling to your wild flesh and weep. Oh Babylon, how did we get so old and so fucking afraid of every evangelical fool?*

THE OBITUARY

In her 65th year, she cornered me in at a conference and babbled and sweated. Then she excoriated me twelve months later in print for my useless and limited fame. Five years later, I saw her at K-Mart, but by then I'd learned to be invisible. Unseen, I watched her raccoon eyes sparkle, shimmering in the wake and shake of ethereal madness and demented consumerism. She wore ancient cat-eye glasses and sported a hairdo made of yellow-gray straw. Oh my god, her pubic hair must have been straw too! She didn't live poems; she constructed them. She was a builder, not quite a formalist, but a strange karaoke elder, a master of screed. I was a drooling destroyer. She had nearly eighteen years on me, but we were both stranded on the shores of a strange and dangerous country. We were equally lost on the red road. Our wisdom was simply weariness with wildness. When our common became arcane, we kneeled to the most convenient God. We called this prostration poetry, but her fingers had lost their acuity. Mine still have not. They curl into fists and exact this sad revenge. And I don't know if I win or lose, but I do feel slight groin tremors right now when I scan her obituary. In her coffin, I hope she feels these shivers of joy, pain, and relief, this slow release of deliciously stinky sex syrup.

THE DAY THE JETS KISSED TWIN TOWERS

The horn-rimmed, zit-faced farm boy computing my bill at Morlock Ford smiled as he mishandled and then dropped a page fast-fed by laser printer. "Lots of exhaust fumes in this dump," I said. He nodded, muttered, "You just accept the buzz and go on with your work." I stared into his smiling eyes, his cheap-thrill heaven, and flash-danced back to 1967 until he turned on the tube. In this ersatz world, this CNN reality that I'm too old to bark at, I could only shrug. Eternal-sperm-for-brains-me—I'm now past fifty but sometimes talk to my mirror-self like I was a young stud in bell-bottoms. *It's like this, my man.* I can still blabber straight to the ghost of my wild-boy-blood and slobber against Jehovah's perpendiculars. I can still sway an occasional woman and say just the right hoodoo, make any turmoil twitch, but therein lies the problem. When I cast my spell, old, scaly Satan's serpent refuses to strike. And my tongue? Well, it downright refuses to play the game. It remains mute until this now muddled and middle-aged confession. SO, when the jets kissed the Twin Towers that day, I just shuddered like I did that day when I heard that Nixon actually wanted to nuke Vietnam. I paid my repair bill and left. That night the wailing television only made me sleepy. The talking heads wanted me to hate the Arabs, but I really could not. In dreams I saw them ghost-dancing like strange Muslim NDNZ.

LIBERTY STREET

She wore strange spiked hair, but her intent was clear. She was walking it. She was out walking her pussy like some strange dog on a leash. It was pushed out and leading her down the sidewalk. It was a big one. Her tight, white slacks held the beast in bay. Flags were shuddering on every street corner.

When she caught me gawking, she halted, put her hands on hips and stared me down. I turned my eyes from her scornful frown, pushed the sour fear back down my throat and drove deeper into our shivering heartland. That night I bought a flag and blended in with the other sheep.

(September 13, 2001)

POST-TRAUMATIC SKIN DISORDER

I wake at three a.m. and spot a Sticky-Note on a California merlot bottle that says: "No matter where you go, there you are!!!" God, was that a line from a late-night movie? I limp up the stairs, my knee has gone bum this month, and put on Marley's "No Woman, No Cry." Then I enter the realm of my eMac. Via electronic mail some nut I've never met asks about Yeats and his "Second Coming" and how it relates to American Indians and I don't know what to say, the cats are clawing at my toes and the hour is late and I recall earlier watching an Animal Channel show about cats and those cats were making noises and my own cats were going a little gonzo, my new girl cat is just getting out of heat, and I don't suppose any seer anywhere across this nation is thinking anything similar. No matter. What we do on paper matters less and less. The communal eyeballs of the America are being blurred blind by television.

I have nothing to say about Yeats except I love his lampshade poem. And I have nothing to say about Jew-hating Arabs raping the Twin Towers and making every fearful American paste flag upon flag upon flag except all this terrorism shit would not happen if we learned to dialogue with the Muslims like they were our equals. Maybe—if—we admitted as an American nation that the Israelis have become truly Teutonic in their treatment of the Palestinians. Maybe if we admitted that Islam is as valid as Christianity—maybe if we admitted that we *are* a greedy, greasy Nation . . .

Who the Christ knows? All, all, all, ALL I want to do is bathe in the memory of the beautiful Lakota girl I saw today in the neon heaven-shine of the remodeled Safeway store in Chadron, Nebraska. Her tight, bleached t-shirt rose slowly—unintentionally revealing her virginal belly and flawless Sioux skin. If God could've channeled the province of Viagra into my soul, I would have bowed down to her in the confines of my gray and tattered tipi, let her slowly slash my sagging neck and drink my once-warrior blood. Her crimson mouth would have giggled briefly, then scowled as she flounced firmly to the kitchen to grill my buffalo burgers and fries.

for Joel Waters

APPROACHING THE DOUBLE NICKEL

I'm back in Huskerland courting the couch and cable TV. Another school year is over and I'm slowly healing from the incessant Stooge slaps of backwaters academe. I never learn or maybe I am too old now to learn. The springtime of my fifty-fourth year has passed. It's summer vampire time, 3:47 in the a.m., and I'm dancing, listening to "Ragas on Slide Guitar" on the CD player. Outside the thick, night air is filled with grain dust and the screeching of redneck pickup trucks. My cats close the door to my sanctuary because they've seen me dancing and my body is falling apart, and oh, it's all so embarrassing and futile. Earlier today I had four skin tags surgically removed from my neck and I don't want to look at myself, but I'm dancing, doing pretty damn good! Beyond my small town windows, the steaming summer streets of this small town are silent and finally, so am I, except for the tattered red flags of my dead dreams. *Revolución, revolución.* I was so lovely green when I uttered *those* illusions.

RECALLING DAYS OF WINE AND ROSES

I.

I'm helping spoon gruel into you at the nursing home when you decide to fall asleep. I shake your shoulder and break loose an ancient memory. Sweetheart, can you recall that time twenty years ago when I crawled back home to the Rez cross-eyed drunk, stinking of some toothless skank I pawed and French-kissed at the Indian bar in Gordon, Nebraska. You cried and it was rain-snowing and I went outside in a show of macho lunacy and just stood there for twenty-five minutes until your heart softened and you sang the softest NDN song and called me back in. I kissed you desperately and then I cooked eggs and fried potatoes with jalapeños, all mixed together . . . you were asleep by the time I plated them and before I knew it, so was I, on the floor where you awakened me to a ravenous, triple-Tylenol Pine Ridge sunrise.

II.

I made it here from Minnesota in six and a half hours—only two pit stops and one quick whiz right on the interstate outside of primitive Kadoka! You're licking your lips because they took out all your teeth last week and it feels weird. You don't remember. They put you under and I sat in the lobby of the Pine Ridge PHS hospital five hours waiting. Colleen, now you look like Granny on re-runs of the "Beverly Hillbillies," but you told me something similar twelve years ago when I had mine yanked. Now you can't eat nothing but *wojapi*! Come here, sweetheart, let us toothless critters kiss, then we'll go smoke a Marlboro. I gotta head back in the morning and it looks like nasty rain is coming. Hey, remember that June '85 night of the 105-degree thunderstorm? How we got nearly naked in our Pine Ridge backyard and shampooed our heads with Ivory dish soap? We were piss-drunk, in the tail end of youth. For sure we did not give a shit, and the nasal whine of Dylan's "Like A Rolling Stone" inhabited our K-Mart stereo. Do you remember, baby? No, of course you don't. Most days now you don't even remember who the hell I am. Most days I don't either.

FOR THE BLACK HORSE OF MY DEATH

Won't you lend your lungs to me?
Mine are collapsing.
Plant my feet and bitterly breathe
up the time that's passing.

— TOWNES VAN ZANDT

I spray Orange-Glo along the length of the long oak table I got half-price from Ufkin's Furniture in Minneota, Minnesota four years ago because one end was almost dinged beyond salvation. I repaired it with love and patience and it looks okay to me and my tomcat, Gerbit, who contemplates his feline mid-age and lack of balls. He sits on the table and screeches to be let out. The thunder is racking this ancient farmhouse. I stare into his eyes and insert a thumb into each ear and wiggle the remaining digits and stick my tongue out. He keeps whining so I let him out into the *raga* of the thunderstorm and go to bed. I snore and wake, wake and snore, brain-fog-dreaming about the beautiful black ghost horse I found standing next to my ancient Ford in the Morlock Super-Grocery parking lot this afternoon. I went back into the store and bought a long dog leash and tied the leash to my car and towed the dark mare home.

After I led her into my house, I raked my fingernails down her flanks like chalk on the screeching blackboard of my senile profession. Dark horse, I've dreamed of the Ghost Dance my whole life. Earlier this cold day I actually grabbed my fat, old man-cat and smooched him on his lips and whispered your name. *Death.* Oh beautiful creature. *Death,* why you've come from faraway buffalo country to do whatever it is you were doing in this moribund Minnesota town is beyond me. Never mind, horse, just let your ears swallow my tears. Allow me to bow down and clean your hooves. Let me paint them the brightest red my life can conjure. The red of carnal sunset. The red of vampire floss. The bullet hole red of my dead desert ancestors.

You made me lie on my back on my dog-stained carpet. You planted both of your front hooves on my tired forehead. You stood there, poised, and balanced until you sank into the soft slime of my brain and silenced my desperate fantasies. Then you walked out the door. Now that you've cantered away, I want to stroke you again, but I probably won't for some years to come. I wish I could sing you a song of thanks. I wish I could sing anything now. I would sing so that I might sleep. I would sing like Sinatra. I would sing Rabbit Dance songs to my shadow. I would sing like the one true love of my life sang before she drooled and stumbled into dementia. I would sing myself once more towards the deep spirit love I know only brown women can give. Black horse, I would sing a smiling song of the sweet, dark dream I will ride you into some morning.

for Simon

CHRISTMAS DAY 2003 IN NEBRASKA

On my way home after rubbery turkey with Colleen at the nursing home, I stop for supplies. The clerk at the Pump & Pantry in Cowturdville teases me about my purchase of Cheez-Puffs, Pepsi, Marlboros, and two tins of Vienna sausage. "Oh Geez, I hope that's not your Christmas dinner?" she smiles, and I smile back knowing she'll probably never break free from the trepanning gravity of this small town. "If it is, it will be *très triste*," I tell her and wink and walk out. At home I strip to my shorts, take to the couch, and quickly suck down my feast. And as has been the case in recent years, the opiate of the masses only makes me vaguely weepy.

THAT INDIAN I HATE ARRIVED TODAY

Today is a good day to be a coward. A hot, yellow day of aberrant humidity. A day of sweat and fatigued fans. A day of yellow grass and green dreams. That Indian I hate arrived today. That just barely scraping by Indian. That hockshop hopping Indian. That Indian who decides it's high time to fall off the wagon. That Indian with unpaid bills swarming like killer bees inside his frantic, longhaired head. Yeah, it's that Indian who can't even pay for the white electricity that powers his ancient Apple computer. I sure wish he'd go away and let me contemplate . . . my true lack of power.

Goddamn it, he's eating my last can of soup.

for Harlan Atwater

GHOST DANCE SONG FOR COLLEEN

Driving you back from the doctor's office, I stare out the window and curse the dreary prairie of early spring. Dirty black cows steam and slog through mud paths in the snow. In a few weeks they will drop calves onto this colorless, desolate world. An hour earlier, a young, manly woman doctor made me wonder why she would take a job among the obscure rednecks of Chadron, Nebraska. I bit my lip and refused to believe her when she said she doubted you'd make it to the warm days of High Plains summer.

My love, we always believed in the Ghost Dance. Put your curled claw of a hand in mine. Let's move into the shimmy line. Circle, circle, we'll soon be fine, spinning towards loving oblivion, Elysium, the ghost road, home.

ABOUT THE AUTHOR

A half-breed Indian, Adrian C. Louis was born and raised in northern Nevada and is an enrolled member of the Lovelock Paiute Tribe. From 1984-97, he taught at Oglala Lakota College on the Pine Ridge Reservation of South Dakota. Prior to this, Adrian C. Louis edited four Native newspapers, including a stint as managing editor of *The Lakota Times* and later *Indian Country Today.* Since 1999 he has been an English professor in the Minnesota State University system.

Adrian C. Louis has written a dozen books of poems including *Fire Water World,* winner of the 1989 Poetry Center Award from San Francisco State University. He has written two works of fiction: *Wild Indians & Other Creatures,* a collection of short stories, and *Skins,* a novel. *Skins* was produced as a feature film, directed by Chris Eyre, and had its national theatrical release in the summer of 2002.

Adrian C. Louis has won numerous writing awards including a Pushcart Prize and fellowships from the Bush Foundation, the National Endowment for the Arts, and the Lila Wallace-Reader's Digest Foundation.